YOU MUST BE A JONES

"A Family Memoir"

Lydia Jones Cole

YOU MUST BE A JONES

"A FAMILY MEMOIR"

LYDIA JONES COLE

NDP

NEW DEGREE PRESS

YOU MUST BE A JONES
A Family Memoir

ISBN 978-1-63676-602-7 *Paperback*
978-1-63676-260-9 *Kindle Ebook*
978-1-63676-261-6 *Ebook*

For my parents, Idabel Greene Jones and George Mason Jones, Sr., who gave me life, love and showed me how to navigate life's journey by connecting me to a power greater than myself. Because of you, Dad, I know what a great father looks like, and Mom, each day, I look to your example as the mother I aspire to be.

Table of Contents

Author's Note

When I was twenty-six and just beginning my television career in the late seventies, I lived in a small apartment in the Northwest section of Washington, DC. I became friendly with a beautiful and gregarious African American woman whom I'll call Bridgette. As our friendship grew, we would often hang out at her apartment laughing—she loved to laugh—talking, listening to music, and enjoying a glass of wine. As we got to know each other, I realized some things I naively had never considered. Everyone didn't grow up the same way I did. Getting to know my new friend was the first time I had a personal encounter with someone who grew up with very different influences at home from me.

Most of the time, when we got together, she did the majority of the talking, especially when the discussion was about family. She often shared stories about her mother that I found surprising. Bridgette's mother was a very attractive woman, but different from the image I had of a mother. Her mother performed in local plays that would sometimes go on the road, leaving her husband to raise their two young children.

It was something I couldn't imagine. Those conversations made me think about my life growing up and how different it might have been from some of my peers. Each time I heard these stories, I just listened.

One day when we were hanging out, Bridgette asked, "Why don't you ever talk about your family?"

My response was, "There isn't much to say. Talking about my family would be like hearing about the Waltons—boring."

It may sound like an oxymoron to compare growing up as a child in an all-Black neighborhood in the 1950s and 1960s in Arlington, Virginia, and the Walton family from the popular 1970s television show. But that's what it felt like. How could I envision my family being anything like the Waltons? I grew up in Virginia when the state and most of the country was segregated and would continue to be until the mid-60s. Could African Americans in the early part of the twentieth century truly live a wholesome, positive home life even with all the institutional constraints imposed upon us in the first part of the twentieth century?

Growing up on Hall's Hill until the early 60s, we didn't have full access to Arlington's hospitals, we couldn't sit at the lunch counter in the local drugstore or attend movie theaters in Arlington, and segregation separated our schools. The restrictions imposed on African Americans, shaped by racist policies and reinforced by media, were meant to limit and stifle our community, literally and figuratively.

The white communities that surrounded Hall's Hill mounted intentional efforts to move African Americans out of our neighborhoods. We were seen as undesirable people, living on highly sought-after property. But our homes had less value as long as we occupied them. And we were automatically considered to be poor.

But we didn't feel poor, we didn't feel less smart, less interesting, or less of anything. And, there was no yearning to crossover—to be white. In fact, those thoughts never entered my mind growing up.

The limitations created by segregation were burdensome, but they did not define us, and we did not allow them to limit us.

The comparison of my family to the Waltons wasn't about a white family living in the mountains of Virginia. It was the wholesomeness of their lives and their large, close-knit family that reminded me of my own. My family had the same Waltons energy, camaraderie, and healthy bit of rivalry among sisters and brothers. And our closeness and unity extended beyond our immediate family to grandparents, aunts, and uncles—all who lived within walking distance of our home. We ate dinner as a family on Sundays, went to church together, we helped each other with homework, and we all felt a sense of accomplishment when our oldest brother was the first in our immediate family to go to college.

When I thought about my mother, it wasn't her looks that made her different. She was a pretty woman, simple yet classic, with little interest in baubles and adornment, not inclined to wear makeup other than a classic but understated red lipstick. Her attire was traditional, and she had little interest in entertainment other than television. Her focus was her kids and husband, her home, her faith, and her community.

Years after those conversations with Bridgette, I conducted genealogical and historical research on my community, and I came across a blog post about Hall's Hill. I was surprised to see a blog about my neighborhood, written by a white woman. The narrative was offensive, racist, and a searing reminder of how white people in Arlington viewed Black people.

An excerpt from her blog described our community like this:

"And Hall's Hill was just around the corner, down Lee Highway. Hall's Hill was where we kept all of our colored folk in Arlington, Virginia in the fifties. Al's Bar and Grill was at the top end where you could see it and there was never any reason to go down any of the other streets. Northern Virginia is more cosmopolitan than the rest of Virginia: I don't remember seeing any helpful signs on the drinking fountains to let you know what color water you were dealing with. Mostly, we did without that sort of thing, because we had all the colored people bunched up in Hall's Hill all neat and tidy, and all we had to do then was zone things around it. So there was a colored school, and there were Regular schools, and that was that. You were assigned based on your address alone, and it worked out just fine without anybody having to spell it out. Sometimes there were slipups. I do remember we couldn't get into the Overlee swimming pool because our house was stuck like a scab on the edge of Hall's Hill and we were zoned out. . . . Anyway, I did some checking, and it turns out Hall's Hill was the first place they established for freed slaves at the end of the Civil War, and their descendants stayed put for a good hundred years. They didn't start leaking out until just about the time I went away to college, and I haven't been back."

After reading this abhorrent description of Hall's Hill, I knew I needed to tell my family's story.

The blogger claims her writings are satirical. But I knew they were, for the most part, an actual reflection of what she and her family thought of our community and everyone who lived there. Her joking reference to zoning was not some made-up thing; it was real. Arlington County instituted zoning regulations that limited residents of Hall's Hill.

Private homeowners created barriers to segregate their property from ours, limiting entrances and access to our neighborhood. In the 1930s, white homeowners built one continuous wall on the southern and eastern ends of Hall's Hill. The eastern portion of the wall separated all Black homes on Culpepper and Buchannan Streets from white homes. On the southern, the wall separated Black families from whites on Culpepper, Cameron, and Dinwiddie Streets, eliminating all southern exits from our neighborhood.[1]

My story is not the narrative often shared about Black folk's lives in historically African American communities all across this country. It deviates from those written about the Great Migration of African Americans moving to the North in search of a better life. Hall's Hill is where many free Black people and newly freed slaves put down roots in the late 1800s, and generations stayed for more than a century.

The sense of home and familiarity among us may have emanated from multiple generations of families remaining in Hall's Hill. Neighbors depended on each other and supported each other. In some small way, the entire community contributed to our upbringing, making the African proverb, "It takes a village to raise a child," our reality.

Growing up on Hall's Hill felt safe, you felt loved, and you knew you mattered.

Inside the Jones household, our parents seemed strict and rigid. Still, as adults, we all recognize the priceless rewards we

1 John Liebertz, *A Guide to African American Heritage of Arlington County, Virginia*, (Arlington: Arlington Department of Community Planning, Housing and Development Historic Preservation Program, 2016), p. 22.

gained: learning what real love looks and feels like and being accepted as an individual while learning how to get along. We learned to appreciate diverse personalities, understand the importance of a spiritual relationship, the value of education, perseverance, and the benefits of a strong work ethic.

You Must Be A Jones shines a light on the real-life ups and downs of Black family life that rarely are told. My family life was not an anomaly. There were communities just like ours all over the country. All African American children don't grow up in homes where parents are absent, on drugs, living in poverty, or dealing with the hardships of social challenges. But we rarely hear those stories.

My parents were my protectors, my confidence builders, my examples of how to live a happy and fulfilled life, never having to prove my worth to anyone. Sadly, in the twenty-first century, this look-back through my family's life may be more vital than anticipated. America was literally built upon devaluing African Americans as a people, and in 2020 we again recognize that some Americans still cling to that belief and want nothing more than to turn back the hands of time.

If you feel like America has become a place you no longer recognize, reading *You Must Be A Jones*, takes you back in time and shares my family's story on how we lived through some of America's darker periods. Despite that reality, we experienced an ideal childhood and became confident, happy, and successful adults who are intent on repeating that history with our children and grandchildren.

CHAPTER 1

Giving Thanks

Thanksgiving 2018 was the first time our family gathered for a holiday without Mom or Dad. It was also my year to host our family dinner. Typically, this was a responsibility I eagerly took on. I really enjoy cooking. It doesn't get any better than preparing great food on Thanksgiving for people you love. I enjoy shopping for the best foods and ingredients and blending them to create one incredible meal that our family can't get enough of. There's nothing about it that I don't like—finding the best recipes, cooking, and buying flowers to make the house bright and cheerful.

That year, without Mom and Dad to dote on, to cater to, to be with us, well, I didn't know how it would feel. Would there be an air of sadness? Would the typical kinetic energy of our family's most important get-together be gone? Would being together without our parents' physical presence be enough to make Thanksgiving as memorable as always? Only time would tell.

Our Jones family Thanksgiving dinners were never stuffy or formal. There was no air of pretense, no matter who was hosting dinner. You could count on all the little cousins finding a corner to gather in or making their way to the basement to laugh and play games. As long as no one got hurt, they were free to play and revel in just being together again.

For the adults, it was a chance to catch up on what we had been up to since we last saw each other. There were rarely earthshaking conversations. In between helping the host with any last-minute tasks, generally, we talked about our kids, our jobs, and congratulated nieces and nephews on their accomplishments. If anyone happened to be miffed with anyone else—which didn't happen very often—they knew not to bring it to Thanksgiving. It just wasn't the kind of thing our family did. Whatever the issue, we found a way to work it out amicably. That's how Mom and Dad raised us.

Our family is big, so there were always lots of people and lots of activity. There are seven children in our immediate family, most have spouses, grown children, and some of us have grandchildren. A typical Thanksgiving dinner for the past twenty years meant twenty-five to thirty people of all ages. Six of us rotated who would host, a practice we have been following since we outgrew the 900-square-foot house in which we grew up.

Either my siblings George Mason, Michael, Rosalind, Audrey, Wilma, or I hosted dinner on Thanksgiving. And the seventh sibling, my twin brother Lynwood and his wife Jacqueline, always drove up from North Carolina to Washington, Maryland, or Northern Virginia for the Thanksgiving holiday.

The year before, in 2017, we had dinner at my sister Wilma's house in Arlington. Before we sat down to eat, and as some of us were still arriving, our mother became ill and was rushed to the hospital. It was frightening and unthinkable all at once.

Twenty-five family members had gathered at Wilma's house for Thanksgiving. When we realized Mom would not be leaving the hospital, the doctor gave her medication to relieve her pain. She went into a deep sleep before being moved to a room where all the family members gathered. My mother's children, grandchildren, and great-grandchildren surrounded her in her last hours. Twenty-five of us stayed with her to say our final goodbyes. It's unlikely that there would have been any other day where we were all together like we were every Thanksgiving.

Just six months earlier, on May 6, we had celebrated Mom's ninety-fifth birthday with a surprise luncheon at RT's in Alexandria, Virginia. RT's was a popular local restaurant with great Cajun and Creole food. The backroom at RT's made it a perfect location for Mom's birthday. The front of the restaurant was quaint and filled with booths and a large bar. There was a separate seating area with plenty of space for us all and a few extra tables along the sides to the right of the front door. It was sufficiently private, so the little kids could walk around the room without disturbing any other tables or customers. We needed the space. It was a full house.

Almost everyone came—all of my brothers and sisters, along with our significant others. Most of Mom's grandchildren and most of her great-grandchildren were there. There were almost as many of us at Mom's ninety-fifth birthday as there were at our traditional Thanksgiving Day celebration.

Special doesn't aptly describe the day. Dad had died on January 17, 2014, sixteen days before his ninety-fifth birthday. Mom's celebration would have been important no matter what, but the day was even more memorable because we didn't get to celebrate that milestone with Dad. This was time to savor—time to show Mom how important she was to each of us. To say thank you in the most personal way, over a meal with people you love and those who love you back.

I don't recall if Mom was completely surprised by the luncheon, but I could see the happiness in her face as she looked around the room. Her smile conveyed it all. And Roz's husband, an excellent photographer, captured that moment with a group photo of everyone. Michael Harris had been cataloging our family gatherings for more than thirty years. That day, he took the most amazing picture. Later he had it blown up, framed, and gave it to my mother to hang on the wall in her living room. It was impossible not to be drawn to it.

After my mother passed, I asked Roz if Michael could have a copy of the picture made for me. Several of my siblings already had one, so Roz told me to take the photo from Mom's house. It's a captivating picture. Whenever someone sees it hanging on the wall in my house, they ask, "Who is this?" We're all smiling from ear to ear, gathered around Mom, who has Aliya, one of her great-grandchildren, on her lap. At ninety-five, you could still see life in her smile. Despite arthritis in her legs and her mild case of high blood pressure, she rarely complained about any ache or pain.

It was one reason Roz knew something had to be very wrong the night Mom fell ill. She was in a lot of pain, and she told the doctor who examined her that Thanksgiving night. "Before I fainted, I was not in any pain," Mom said to the emergency room physician.

Mom had delivered seven children, including a set of twins, and never had an epidural or any pain medication.

Roz would always say, "Mom has a high tolerance for pain."

My mother's aorta, her main artery had ruptured, and within a few hours after she arrived at the hospital, she had passed.

This year, our first without Mom and Dad needed to be extra special. I wasn't sure how to do that. In the weeks leading up to the holiday, I felt a sense of trepidation. I wondered to myself, Why did I agree to host Thanksgiving this year? Would I disappoint my family? Would I disappoint myself? I shared my feelings with my husband, Reg.

He assured, "It will be fine. Just do what you always do, and it will work out fine."

Would the memory of our last Thanksgiving make the day difficult? How could it not? I was hoping, somehow, to create an atmosphere where everyone felt happiness, and a sense of belonging, like every other Thanksgiving we had shared. But I didn't know. All I could do was pray and ask God to give us the strength to find joy in the good life that our mom, Idabel Greene Jones, and our dad, George Mason Jones Sr., had instilled in each of us.

An apt description for our parents might be "salt of the earth" type of people. The Bible verse, "Do unto others as I would have them do unto you," wasn't just scripture. It was how they lived their life and how they taught us to treat others. On this day, I prayed our faith and love for each other would help us honor our parents by giving thanks as if they were there beside us.

In the weeks leading up to Thanksgiving, I spent hours creating a schedule that detailed everything I needed to do for the holiday dinner. Reg and I talked about how we would divide and conquer to get the house ready. When it came to having company over, Reg could sometimes be more persnickety than me. Would there be enough seating? Should we put folding tables up? Where should the children eat? He decided it would be best to put the kids in the basement. There was plenty of room for them to sit at folding tables. They could watch television and move around freely.

I organized my cleaning regimen and plotted out exactly which room I would clean up and when. I cleaned the refrigerator the week before dinner to make room for the large amount of food I needed to purchase. I decided to add gumbo to the menu. I never prepare gumbo on Thanksgiving. It's a dish that takes a lot of time. But this year was different. I was going all out.

I was determined to get it right. That meant I needed to cook the gumbo far in advance, so all I had to do was warm it up for Thanksgiving dinner. The weekend before the holiday, I finished my grocery shopping, ordered a fresh organic turkey, prepared seafood gumbo, and placed everything in the refrigerator.

A few last-minute details still needed to be handled. I made sure the tablecloths were clean and identified placemats for the TV tables. Then, I counted and inspected the dinnerware for chips and cracks. The last thing on my list was to pick up Mom's silverware and Audrey's chafing pans from her house. Our daughters, Iman and Maya, and their boyfriends arrived in town the day before Thanksgiving. Both girls know how to cook, and they would be a big help in the final hours before dinner.

As the host, I was responsible for the turkey and any side dishes I chose. The rest of the food would be cooked and brought by my siblings. Iman helped me set the table. Maya made vegan lemon bars. I put the twenty-pound turkey in the oven the night before and set the timer. Before going to bed, I mixed the ingredients for the cornbread stuffing and set it aside. Iman cut up the garlic and Brussels sprouts and grated the parmesan cheese for the dish we would cook tomorrow. She placed the ingredients and the cornbread stuffing in the refrigerator. The turkey would be ready tomorrow morning, freeing up the oven for everything else.

It was late. I was exhausted from standing on my feet all day and ready to go to bed. Throughout the night, I could smell the turkey cooking from my upstairs bedroom. Still, I was worried I would burn up the main course or the house. I had never cooked anything overnight, but it was the only way to be sure everything would be ready on time. Every couple of hours, I awoke to fragrant smells coming from the kitchen. I couldn't take a chance. Periodically, I went down to the kitchen, turned the oven light on, and peeped in. Each time, everything was going as planned.

By 6 a.m., I was up and back in the kitchen. I removed the turkey from the oven. It looked delicious. I resisted cutting a piece, covered it with aluminum foil, and began warming up the gumbo. Iman cooked the Brussels sprouts when she awoke and joined me in the kitchen. Reg prepared the rice for the gumbo. I am a good cook, but the rice is not my forte. I also cooked a leg of lamb, which had been seasoned and placed in the refrigerator the night before. When the turkey came out, the lamb went into the oven.

Not everyone in the family was a fan of lamb, but my mom loved it, as do I. Growing up, Dad would occasionally buy lamb chops for Mom. There was never anything in the refrigerator that we could not eat except Mom's lamb chops.

Lamb chops were expensive and not affordable to feed a family of nine or seven or five or whatever the number of people that lived in our home at the time. But Dad would buy them as a special treat for Mom. I don't recall ever tasting those lamb chops when I was growing up. When I had a chance to try lamb at my friend Lynn's house, I loved it. Whenever I had an opportunity to prepare it for my Mom, I did.

Dinner was at three in the afternoon. Once the doorbell started ringing around two, there was a continuous flow of people for the next thirty to forty minutes. For a change, my portion of the dinner was ready. No matter how early I started preparing for a special dinner, somehow, I was usually late. Not this year! After all these years, I'm sure everyone expected dinner to be late. But no one ever commented about it anymore, at least not to me.

As everyone arrived, they brought their dish with them. The house was already smelling amazing from the roast turkey, gumbo, and lamb. With each new menu item that came in, the aroma only got better. Roz brought ham, Mike brought fish, and Audrey brought chitterlings, which she and George Mason enjoyed, just like my dad did when he was alive. (Chitterlings, not a dish many people eat these days, are the intestines of hogs, which probably sounds pretty disgusting for many people. But when they are cleaned and cooked correctly, they taste pretty good. Chitterlings, or chitlins as some people call them, became a food African Americans initially ate out of necessity during slavery. Enslaved people were fed the scraps from their enslaver's meals. The leftovers from the hog included trotters (feet), maw (stomach), and chitlins.)[2]

---

2 Rachel Rummel, "Chitlins," Atlas Obscura, accessed September 19, 2020.

There were loads of side dishes, collard greens, string beans, sweet potatoes, corn pudding, eggplant parmesan—a filling meal for the family's vegetarians. And there were way too many desserts. Roz treated us to the lemon pound cake my mother always made for special occasions. It was the best. Rich and buttery. Lemony inside and out. There was no icing, just a coating of grated lemon zest, simple sugar, and lemon juice poured on top while the cake was still warm from the oven.

Thanksgiving weather in Washington is unpredictable—often warm, possibly into the low seventies, and other times, snowing. This day was cold and cloudy. There would be lots of heavy coats and hats to hang up. Fortunately, we had remembered to remove many of our belongings from the hallway closet to make room for family members' coats. As everyone began to arrive, it was apparent that the overcast day had not crept into their psyche. There were lots of smiles and warm greetings.

As everyone came into the house, either Reg or I took their coats, asked them to remove their shoes, and handed them a pair of footies. Most family members had not been to our house. We had just moved in last year, the week before Thanksgiving. Our home had beige wall-to-wall carpeting in most areas, which we wanted to keep as clean as possible. There would likely be at least thirty people moving around the house for the next several hours. No one resisted. We gave each family member a mini tour of our home, offered them something to drink, and showed them where the remote control was as we prepared for dinner.

Each year before we sat down to eat, when Dad and Mom were alive, we would all hold hands and ask God to bless our gathering and the food. George Mason gave the prayer. As our oldest brother and Dad's namesake, George Mason was the perfect person to put our minds and hearts in the right place as we sat down to enjoy our meal. It wasn't that he was ultra-religious, but he was the elder. We all looked up to him, and at that moment, he deftly became the head of the Joneses—no one needed to say a word. It was his role now. He knew it, and he stepped into his place that evening.

There was no sadness in the air or on anyone's face that day. It was one of our most joyful Thanksgivings. That's significant since I can't remember ever having a family Thanksgiving that wasn't fun.

No one left before nine that night. The love and closeness were palpable in every room throughout the house. At the end of the evening, as is traditional, Roz's husband, Michael, took a group photo. We had thirty-nine people for Thanksgiving.

Our dinner and the entire day said so much about how our parents raised us. What they taught us was not fleeting. It wasn't going away because they were no longer with us. It was us. We could feel and see the realization of everything they worked throughout their lives to instill in us, and we knew we would pass it on to our children and grandchildren.

The Jones family poses for their Thanksgiving 2006 photo.

Mom and Dad's influence even touched some of our neighbors. At their funerals, we realized just how many people outside our family Mom and Dad had affected. Dad was healthy and still active until he was about ninety-three years old when he got dehydrated from being out on an unusually hot day. After being hospitalized, he never regained the energy or ability to get out and about as he had done his entire life. He died after having a heart attack.

Dad's funeral was at his beloved Calloway Methodist Church, the first church established on Hall's Hill in 1866. As we got up and turned to leave the service, we were amazed. The church was full, with only standing room in the worship area and people seated in an overflow area in the basement. It felt good to have so many come out to honor our father's life. Even after the funeral, it made me feel proud to read comments on a Facebook post thanking people for their kindness during Dad's passing. Several young men who grew up in our neighborhood commented on the impact Dad had on their lives. I had no idea he had touched the lives of so many young men.

My mother's funeral was at the church she attended in Washington, DC. Much like Dad's funeral, all the seats were full, with folding chairs placed next to each pew for additional seating. Many people came to offer their condolences, including those who made the forty-five-minute drive from Arlington. A young person who came to pay their respects remarked that they had never seen a funeral for a ninety-year-old person attended by so many people.

My parents ended their lives the way they started them. Humble, full of gratitude, and devoted to their family and their faith.

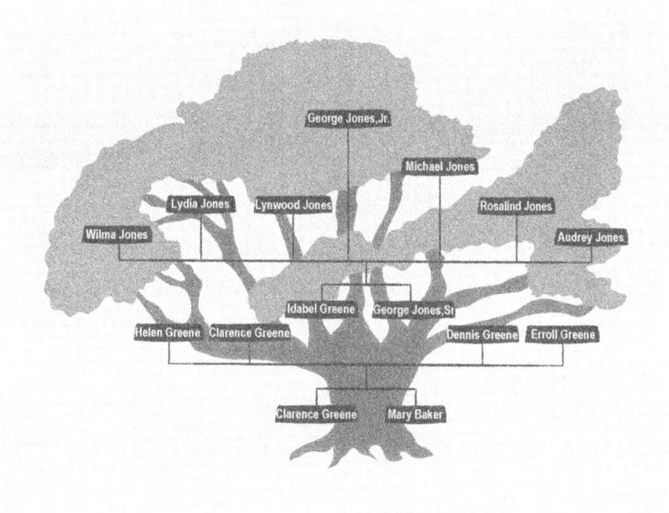

Greene Family Tree

CHAPTER 2

The Greene Family

"We lived here in Hall's Hill, as it was called back then," my mother said as she reflected on her early life.

"It's where I was born. Before my father died, we moved from Hall's Hill because he wanted to have a farm. First, we moved to Forestville and then to Branchville. And while we were in Branchville, that's where he died."

My mother, Idabel Greene, was the youngest of five children. Before her family moved to the farm in Maryland, her parents, Mary Baker Greene and Clarence Greene, lived at 2220 North Frederick Street in Arlington, Virginia, a street that no longer exists on Hall's Hill or Highview Park, the community's current name. For Black people in 1920, my mother's parents had a pretty good life. They were far from rich, but they were not poor.

My grandfather worked as a janitor at the Government Printing Office in Washington, DC. A job in the federal government was, and still is, a stable position with good pay, benefits, and more security than many jobs. When the stock market crashed in 1929, the Great Depression made life for

Black people even worse. Many Black people were laid off, in some cases, to free up jobs for white people. My grandfather was one of the lucky ones. His employment continued. My grandparents were fortunate enough to have a home and the resources to provide for their family well enough that my grandmother could stay home to care for their five children: Helen, Clarence, Dennis, Erroll, and Idabel.[3]

The Greene family's Arlington home was a two-story, three-bedroom house with a front porch extending around one side. By the time my brothers and sisters and I came along, we rarely entered the house through the front door, but the hallway was always dimly lit when we did. It wasn't a large house. To the right of the stairwell, just beyond the front door, was the living room. Further down the hallway, the house became brighter. Sunshine seemed to pour in from all sides at the end of the hallway, where there was a small alcove across from the formal dining room. And a sun-filled kitchen was just beyond the alcove. The hallway continued past the kitchen to the back door, which was how we entered the house.

By 1930, the family had moved to a farm in Maryland. My mother doesn't know why my grandfather wanted a farm, but a look at the 1900 census may hold some clues. When my grandfather was fourteen years old, his father, two brothers, and sister lived on a farm. It's possible he wanted to emulate his dad. While we may never know why they moved, his dream was short lived.

As my mother recalled her father's death, her voice slightly cracked, and she looked away as if to hold back her

3 United States Legislative Information, *Race Relations in the 1930s and 1940s*, Library of Congress, accessed October 1, 2020.

emotions. "He was putting gas in his car, and he had a lantern, and somehow it caught on fire. He tried to pull the car out of the garage, and he got burned. He died within a week after that at Providence Hospital. That changed me a whole lot. It made me realize that I had to grow up without a father. He was a big part of my life. But I got through it with Mama."

My grandfather died on April 26, 1931. Our grandmother, who all the grandchildren called Nana, had been a housewife. Her limited work experience consisted of washing white people's laundry. Mom recalled the financial uncertainty Nana faced after the death of my grandfather. "We didn't have enough money. Mama struggled. I was eight years old, my sister Beanie was nine, Dennis was eleven, Clarence was twelve, and my oldest sister, Helen, was fifteen. Mama had her hands full." My grandmother knew she needed to move her family back to Arlington.

Nana moved the family to Hall's Hill's familiar surroundings among neighbors and friends who knew them and cared about them. Her best friends, Edgie and Sam Harrington, had purchased their home when they moved to Maryland, and they agreed to sell it back to my grandmother.

People who lived on Hall's Hill back then often reminisce about how they looked out for each other. That sentiment continued for many generations. In 2018, during the one-hundred-year celebration of Fire Station 8 on Hall's Hill, a 1940s-era volunteer fireman put it this way: "All we had was each other, so we all helped each other when we were in need."

My grandfather's death was a tragedy for my mother and her family. The void left by his death was challenging enough, but without much money, the future looked pretty bleak.

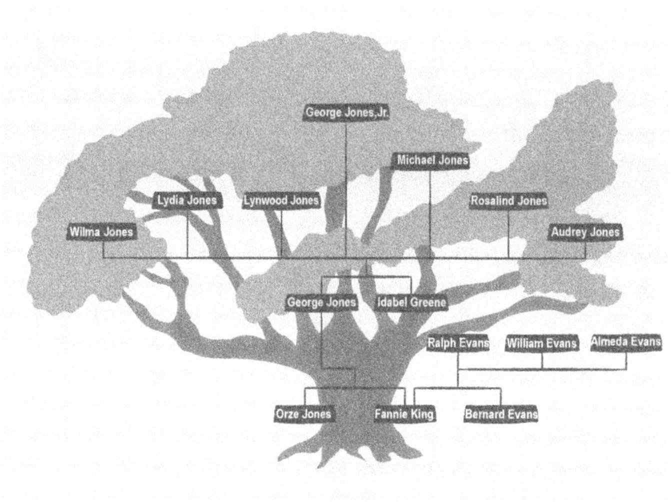

Jones Family Tree

CHAPTER 3

The Joneses

By the time Mom's family moved back to Hall's Hill, my dad, George Jones, was eleven years old. Dad's family lived at 1925 N Edison Street. My grandmother, Fannie Jones, whom we called Grandma Jones, and our grandfather, Orze Jones' house, was a ten-minute walk from where Mom lived. Two streets over and four blocks down from Frederick Street. Many years would pass before our mother and father really got to know each other.

Before marrying Orze Jones, our grandmother was married to Bernard Evans. Fannie and Bernard Evans lived in Washington, DC, and they had three children: Ralph born in 1902, William in 1905, and Almeda in 1907. Bernard died in 1910, and Grandma Jones moved back to Arlington, where she was born.

She returned to Arlington, thirty-six years old, a widow, and with three kids to raise. It made sense to go home, especially with her mother and Aunt Ida still there. Her mother, Elizabeth King, had been a slave in Norfolk, Virginia. After receiving her freedom, she ended up in Arlington. We don't know if she had a specific destination in mind, but once she arrived, she stayed, got married, and began her family as a free woman.[4]

When Grandma Jones returned to Arlington, she bought a small house on Hall's Hill and continued raising her three children. Dad later grew up in that house. It was a narrow, frame building on a twenty-five-foot lot. There were no frills, only the bare necessities—one bedroom, a dining room, kitchen, and bathroom. There was a wood-burning stove in the kitchen for cooking, and it helped keep the house warm. The backyard, narrow like the house, had a little shed for storing tools and miscellaneous items. When I think of Grandma Jones' house, it seems like the size of the house and her stature were totally in sync. She was a very petite woman, short, probably five feet tall or less, with a small bone structure, probably weighing about one hundred pounds.

My grandmother remarried sometime between the move to Hall's Hill and the birth of my father. We don't know the exact dates of their marriage. When Dad was born in 1919, our aunt Almeda, whom we called Meme, and William, whom we called Uncle Henry, were still living at my grandmother's house. My uncle Ralph got married the month before Dad was born. Meme was twelve, and Uncle Henry was fourteen. Once Dad started elementary school, he was the only child living at home. Uncle Ralph and Meme had started families of their own, and Uncle Henry was now living independently.

Neither Mom nor Dad grew up in families with wealth, but despite their struggles, Mom's family was a bit better off

4 Wilma Jones, My Halls Hill Family: More Than a Neighborhood, (New Providence: Bowker, October 10, 2018), p.5.

than Dad's. When Dad was fourteen years old, his father died of a cerebral hemorrhage. Faced with another unthinkable loss, Grandma Jones relied on her faith and inner strength to move forward. Grandma Jones and Dad got through the tough times together.

Much like Nana, Grandma Jones did not have the skills to pursue a trade. She supported her family by earning money as a washwoman. They were challenging times, and money was in short supply. Grandma Jones was good with her hands. She did quilting, and she used her sewing skills to repair and patch Dad's clothing when there wasn't money to buy new ones. The patchwork clothing earned Dad the nickname of Patches. In later years, Patches would morph into a fonder nickname, Pap Jones. Through all the loss, Grandma Jones was comforted by knowing that she had her mother and half-sister, whom we called Aunt Ida, just one street away.

My dad didn't know much about his father's family. I don't recall specific stories about my grandfather, but I remember the look on my dad's face when we talked about his father. We might be looking at old pictures or asking him about his dad's name, Orze, because we had never heard that name before. I only remember his face often had a faint smile, and his expression was warm. Like any young person, losing his father was very difficult for my dad.

In some ways, my uncle Ralph probably became a surrogate father to him. Uncle Ralph and my dad didn't look much alike, except they both had a dark complexion. Dad was not quite as tall as Uncle Ralph, who looked to be about six feet tall. Dad was about five feet, nine inches, but they were both thin as young men. Uncle Ralph was seventeen years older than Dad. And Dad was crazy about him.

Dad never considered Uncle Ralph, Uncle Henry, or Meme as half-siblings; they were his brothers and sister, period. Meme lived just up the street from where our family grew up, and Uncle Ralph was one street over. Uncle Henry eventually moved to North Carolina, so we didn't see him or his family often, but we still stayed in touch. My father's siblings, his aunt Ida, her son Earl, and Grandma Jones were all a part of what would become our Jones Family.

CHAPTER 4

Nana's House

Hall's Hill/Highview Park remains a thriving Arlington neighborhood. It sits between Lee Highway on the North, Glebe Road on the East, North 17th Street on the South, and George Mason Drive on the West. It's less than a four-mile drive from Georgetown, the urban Washington, DC, neighborhood across the Potomac River. Crossing the river into Arlington in the early 1900s was like being transported from the city to the country.

Most families on the "Hill"—that's how people who lived there referred to their hometown—had a garden similar to my grandparents. There were fewer homes, bigger yards, and wooded areas all over. Nearly every family had several fruit trees, and some had chickens, horses, and pigs. The land was abundant with strawberry patches and grape groves. Families enjoyed the benefits of farm life, without the intense labor of a working farm.

Backyard gardens helped feed families, especially during lean times. Neighborhood kids played nearby in the densely wooded areas, often picking fruit and berries along the way.

What they didn't eat got cooked and preserved or canned and stored away for the winter months. Central to Hall's Hill's growth and survival was its proximity to the nation's capital, fertile soil, and the community's spirit.

The first Black people to live in what came to be known as Hall's Hill were slaves. The area was part of a three-hundred-and-twenty-seven-acre plantation owned by a merciless slave owner named Bazil Hall. The onset of the Civil War was life changing for everyone, including Virginia's plantation owners. Hall's property, which encompassed the area that became Hall's Hill, was a frequent battleground for Union troops. When the situation became untenable, he temporarily abandoned his plantation.

After President Lincoln issued the Emancipation Proclamation, many slaves like those in Virginia and other Confederate states were freed, including those who worked on Bazil Hall's plantation. (Slaves in the border states of Missouri, Kentucky, Delaware, and Maryland, which had not joined the Confederacy, were not freed.) Hall returned to his property, intent on selling all his acreage to one buyer. His efforts were unsuccessful, forcing him to parcel his land into small plots that he sold one at a time. He sold some land to white men, and then he began selling to Black people.

The first Black people to acquire land on Hall's Hill were the Chinn and Hyson families. On November 9, 1881, they became proud landowners. With land to call their own, a brighter future was within reach. Hundreds of more families would soon join them.[5]

5 John Liebertz, *A Guide to African American Heritage of Arlington County, Virginia*, (Arlington: Department of Community Planning, Housing and Development Historic Preservation Program. Second Edition 2016) p.15.

It would be more than twenty years later before Mary and Clarence Greene's family purchased a home a few blocks away from the Chinn's. Mary Greene, whom we called Nana, and our grandfather, Clarence, became friends with the Chinn family. Settling down in Hall's Hill offered more than a house. It was a chance to build a community of family and friends with shared interests and dreams for a better future.

The Greene family home at 2220 N. Frederick Street in Arlington, Virginia.

The Greenes didn't have family on Hall's Hill when they moved there around 1918, but Nana's mother, Elizabeth, and her husband, George Anderson, lived close. They had moved to Arlington sometime before 1910; they had two sons, Frederick and George. Long before then, fifteen-year-old Elizabeth, whose maiden name was Baker, gave birth to Mary in 1884. She was a teenage mother living with her parents in Warrenton, Virginia. Elizabeth's first child became our Nana.

Nana never knew her father. For years, our family speculated about his identity. Growing up, we always heard that

Nana's father was a Native American, or an Indian, as we used to say. Those stories seemed plausible for all of us. Why wouldn't they? Nana's features—her long straight hair, high cheekbones, long sharp nose, and fair skin—or light skin, as we would say back then, resembled people we thought to be Native American.

After finding an old picture in a family album of a tall, handsome Native American man with long braids wearing traditional Native clothing, we wondered, who is this man? Later I found another picture of Nana's grandmother holding a baby and standing next to a Native American man. The stories had to be true!

Many years later, our brother Mike had Mom's DNA analyzed. Most of us expected some percentage of her DNA to be Native American. No one was more surprised than Mom when she saw the results. All she could say was, "What!" To our disbelief and Mom's amazement, her ethnicity was 56 percent European and 43 percent African. While we still don't know who Nana's father was, we know he was a white man.

My siblings and I have no idea what my grandmother looked like as a young woman. The family albums are devoid of her image. There are pictures of our grandfather, Mom, and our aunts and uncles. Not one picture of Nana. Mom told us, "Mama didn't like anyone to take her picture."

In her sixties, Nana was still a beautiful woman. She was medium height and a little on the heavy side. And she had the most beautiful hair. It was utterly gray, straight, and long, reaching down her back, almost always worn in a bun. One of the few times we saw its full beauty was when she took it down to comb.

Nana was blessed to have grandparents that filled the gap when her mother needed to work away from home. She knew firsthand what it meant to have a supportive family. As Nana moved her five children back to Hall's Hill, she must have felt a tremendous weight knowing their care and support was up to her alone. If returning to domestic work and doing laundry for white people was what was necessary to keep her family clothed and fed, that is what she would do.

By the time Nana reached her seventies, many years of manual labor, working on her knees, and bending over a washboard had started to take their toll on her body. Her legs were swollen and often covered in thick stockings to help soothe the pain. She moved slowly and always needed something to lean on. She kept a cane or a chair nearby to help steady herself when she moved throughout the house.

Home Again

Not long after returning to Hall's Hill, Nana's oldest daughter, Helen, got married in 1933 and moved to Washington, DC, to start her family. Mom's other sister, Aunt Beanie, whose real name was Erroll, followed in her footsteps in 1939. Aunt Beanie—who was very thin, like a string bean growing up, also moved to DC with her husband. Uncle Clarence got married, relocating to DC with his wife. Our mother, Idabel, was the one person consistently at home. Dennis, Uncle Dede to us, still single and living at home, often traveled around the country doing work as part of the Works Progress Administration program (WPA).

President Franklin Roosevelt started the WPA in 1935 to create jobs and relieve the economic hardship so many were suffering during the Great Depression. The program offered work to skilled and unskilled citizens on a variety of projects that ranged from creating parks, building roads, bridges, schools, and other public structures.[6]

In the course of a few years after returning to Hall's Hill, Nana had watched her children blossom into attractive and industrious adults ready to assume their independence. Both Uncle Dede and Uncle Clarence were tall and slim, a little over six feet, and handsome. Uncle Dede, in particular, looked a lot like his father. They both had broad shoulders and excellent posture, almost seeming to stand at attention. Uncle Clarence, who looked a bit more like Nana, was a little taller than Uncle Dede, although he didn't have the same broad shoulders as Uncle Dede and our grandfather.

All three girls, Aunt Helen, Aunt Beanie, and Mom looked like Nana. Each one was about five feet, five or six inches tall. They had long hair and sharp features, but Aunt Beanie was very, very thin, Aunt Helen was slim, and while Mom was closer to Aunt Helen's size, her bone structure was a bit larger.

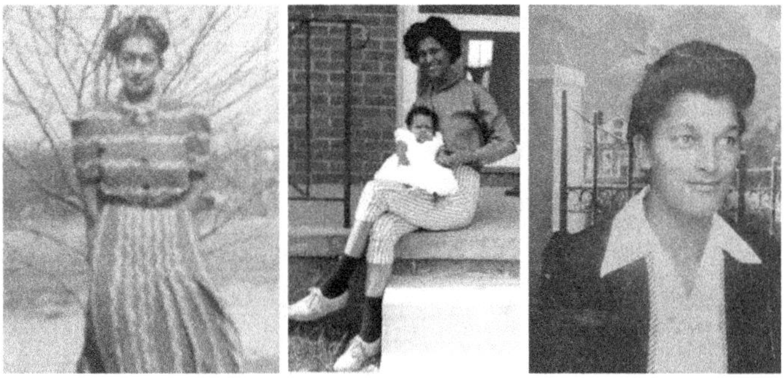

Helen Greene *(left)*, Glovenia Erroll Greene (Aunt Beanie) *(middle)*, Idabel Greene (Mom) *(right)*

6 Library of Congress, *Today in History - April 8: Works Progress Administration*, accessed October 1, 2020.

With primarily Mom and Nana in the house, there were now fewer mouths to feed, but money was still in short supply. The country continued to suffer through the Great Depression, which would last until 1939. Like everything else, the Depression hit African Americans worse than most. Although Mom was the youngest and still in high school, she quit school to work full time to help Nana pay the bills.

"It wasn't long after I left school that I met your father. I knew him all along. He was a cadet. I used to see him coming home in his uniform. Looking all sharp." Mom and Dad knew each other already.

Everybody in Hall's Hill knew everyone else, or they knew of each other's family. One night at a neighborhood party, Mom and Dad got to know each other better.

"We were at a lawn party one night, and we got to talking, and that's how it started. We started dating, and then we got married. I was nineteen, and he was twenty-two." As Mom reminisced about this time, a huge smile came across her face.

Lawn parties were a big deal for young people growing up on Hall's Hill. "Every weekend somebody had a lawn party. That was a big thing. They sold all kinds of food, and they had music. It was more or less like a get-together," Mom said as she recalled her teenage years.

Our parents didn't have a wedding. They drove to Rockville, Maryland, on November 17, 1941, only informing Mom's sister, Aunt Helen, who went with them to witness their nuptials. Possibly because they had discovered Mom was pregnant. Excited to share the news about their recent union, the newlyweds drove home.

Entering the house, they were most likely nervous, but in a good way. Mom proudly announced their marriage to Nana and showed her the marriage license. A cold shoulder and a frown let them know Nana was not pleased. Several days passed before she looked at their marriage license. Mom's sister, Beanie, didn't help matters. She turned up her nose and expressed her displeasure. "I think that's awful," Aunt Beanie said.

But our Aunt Helen was different. Mom adored her oldest sister, and it was easy to understand why. She congratulated the newlyweds and brought them a small wedding cake to celebrate their new beginnings as husband and wife.

Years later, as Mom recalled this story to us, she seemed to understand Nana's reaction in hindsight. "You know, they always want you to marry the best," Mom said. Her family would come to learn—he was the best.

Mom and Dad had planned to rent a room after getting married, but Dede asked her to stay. With his travels around the country, if Mom left, Nana might be alone more often than not. Even though Nana initially made things uncomfortable for Mom and Dad, they decided to start their new life in our grandmother's house. Nana slowly warmed up to Dad. While we don't know for sure how Grandma Jones felt, I believe she was proud of her son for doing what was right.

Before they got married, Dad had planned to return to Minor Teacher's College. He had already completed one semester but dropped out because he didn't have money to buy the clothes he needed for college. The money he earned working as a helper in the machine shop at Washington Navy Yard could help him save to return to college. Dad was good with numbers and had an aptitude for math. His future goal was to become an engineer.

Things were different now with a wife and a baby on the way. Caring for the family was now Dad's priority. Increasing his earning potential was the best way to ensure he would create a better life for his new family.

The Navy Yard had a federal program for people who wanted to become a machinist. It was the first chance Dad had to get ahead. He applied and received a disappointing response that he had missed the program deadline. Only applications submitted within two years after graduation from high school were eligible. They knew there would be other opportunities. As soon-to-be parents, they held onto their faith and belief that better days would be ahead, just like Nana and Grandma Jones.

On March 12, 1942, George Mason Jones Jr. was born. Everyone referred to the new baby as George Mason. He was Mom and Dad's first baby and Nana's fourth grandchild. Mom's sisters, Aunt Beanie and Aunt Helen, already had children. Aunt Helen had two boys, Donald and Luther, and Aunt Beanie had one son, Wesley. But George Mason was the youngest and the only grandchild to live at Nana's house.

Fighting for Freedom?

Before George Mason was two years old, his life and my mother's would drastically change. Dad received his notification of draft into the army on December 4, 1943. For the next two and a half years, Dad was an active-duty soldier. In basic training and in the infantry, he was assigned to the 'colored' troops in Belgium and France fighting to defend democracy in World War II.

There was such hypocrisy in the country's unequal policies and laws. At home, African Americans had to endure substandard living conditions, racial and economic inequities, and unfair hiring practices. But when it was time to fight for the country, we were expected to fight for rights we didn't have at home and to put our lives on the line. Dad, my uncles, and every able-bodied twenty-five to thirty-five-year-old man on Hall's Hill fought in World War II, and some fought in the Korean War.

Segregation was a way of life in America. That included US military units. But segregation was not a part of life in Europe. Black soldiers were free to eat, drink, or patronize the same places as European citizens and residents in the Pacific. In their own country, this same freedom was unavailable to them.

At home, things were not getting easier. Mom and Nana had to keep the family going. The war had exacerbated an already difficult situation. Between my grandfather's death, the Great Depression, and a war that sent all the men in the family to the other side of the world, they were challenging times.

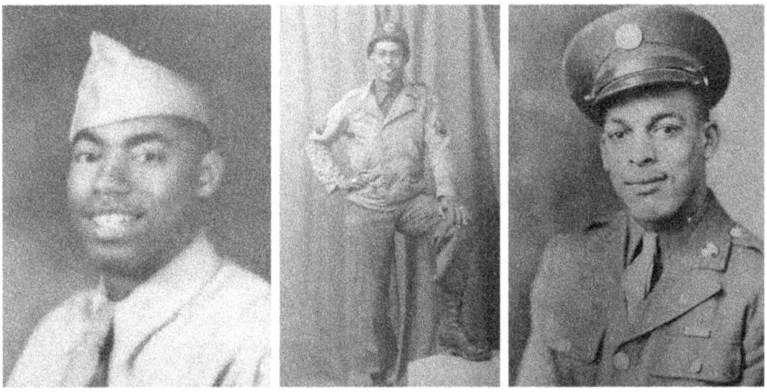

George Jones (Dad) *(left)*, Clarence Greene (Uncle Clarence) *(middle)*, Dennis Greene (Uncle Dede) *(right)*

Mom wasn't much of a worrier—or at least she didn't show it. She held tight to her faith in God to get her family through any trial or tribulation. It's a practice she learned from her mother and father. It seemed they couldn't get a break, but the presence of a toddler raised their spirits and affirmed their belief that better days lie ahead.

During Dad's two-year-plus World War II tour of duty, there were glimmers of progress at home. Mom landed an entry-level clerk job working for the federal government in the public housing department. And Nana took care of George Mason. But no amount of money could shield them from the heartbreak when Aunt Helen contracted pneumonia and died November 16, 1944. She was a twenty-nine-year-old wife and mother of two young children. Her sons, Donald and Luther, would continue to be raised by their father. Both boys visited Nana often until her passing.

The year after Aunt Helen died, Uncle Clarence returned back to the states from the war in November 1945. More than once, Mom and Nana had been able to follow the work of his unit as they helped to rebuild bridges and roads throughout France. The newspaper described their work as "all types of vital construction and repair work." One article even mentioned him by name. Upon his return home, Uncle Clarence went back to work applying and improving his carpentry and construction skills, but his marriage did not survive the separation.[7]

Uncle Dede ended his tour of duty in December 1945. He served for four years fighting at Normandy and earning the American Defense Ribbon, American Theater Ribbon, Europe-Africa-Middle East-Theater (EAMET) Campaign Ribbon with two bronze service stars, Asiatic Pacific Theater Ribbon, Philippine Liberation Ribbon, and Good Conduct

7 *D.C. Sgt. Engineer Foreman in France.*

Medal. In the early part of his deployment, he came down with pneumonia and recovered quickly. Years later, Uncle Dede fell ill again. This time he suffered a lengthy hospitalization, and for a while, his condition was critical. Despite the bleak outlook, Uncle Dede pulled through. We can only imagine the deep sense of relief when the family found out he had improved.

And then the complete diagnosis came. It was Parkinson's Disease. Uncle Dede realized his life would never be the same. The Army refused to acknowledge that Uncle Dede's illness was the result of occurrences during his active duty. He never received service disability benefits, despite having no health issues prior to entering the Army.

I don't know how long it took Uncle Dede's health to improve enough for him to resume some semblance of normalcy in his life, but once it did, he continuously worked until he retired in his sixties. With treatment and daily doses of medicine, he would control the symptoms and effects of the disease. Uncle Dede didn't let Parkinson's cut him off from working and pursuing his interests in photography, gardening, church, and creating innovative solutions for the household. He was still smart, talented, and capable of contributing to society.

When she returned to Hall's Hill, Nana had friends and neighbors she could depend on. She also knew life would not be easy. What she could never have anticipated was the loss of her oldest child, Aunt Helen, and that her son would return from the war with a debilitating condition.

CHAPTER 5

A Home of Our Own

Dad was the last to leave for the war and the last to return home in April 1946. As soon as he arrived home, he wanted to purchase a house for his family. He returned to his job at the Washington Navy Yard, working to make that possible.

Two and a half years was a long time to be separated from his young son and wife. As a four year old, George Mason's recollections of Dad were through the letters Mom read him and the pictures tucked into each envelope. Years later, he thought back on what it felt like to have Dad back home.

"Dad went to work, and I just remember being excited, running back and forth between our driveway to Miss Edgie's and Mr. Sam's house and grabbing pears and fruit off the trees. I was just running around being a kid."

In Nana's house, George Mason was the center of attention, not simply because he was Mom and Dad's only child. Between Nana, Uncle Clarence, and Uncle Dede, there was always someone around with a hug, ready to play ball, or surprise him with candy or a toy. He was attentive to what the adults did, especially Nana.

"Nana was always working around the house, washing clothes on the scrub board, and hanging them outside to dry on the clothesline. For a while, they had chickens and a garden. On Saturday, they prepared for Sunday dinner by grabbing one of the chickens and chopping the head off. Then they would douse the chicken in a tub of hot water and take it to Nana to prepare for our Sunday dinner."

George Mason had less than a year to grab all the attention he could get. By January 19, 1947, he had a baby brother named Michael. Everyone was excited about the new baby, except George Mason. George Mason said, "Everything was great until Mike came."

Dad is holding Mike as George Mason stands behind him.

When George Mason wasn't out playing with his friends, he pouted around the house and yearned for the attention he once had to himself. After several months passed, he sat on the steps of Nana's front porch with Mike in his carriage. He looked sullen and mumbled to himself, "Why is everybody always playing with Mike? What about me? Why are Mama and Daddy are always holding him?"

A split second later, George Mason pushed Mike's carriage down the dirt road. It hit a bump. Up in the air he went. Ouch! Mike hit the ground, and the crying began. The sound of a baby's cry sent Mom running to see what was going on.

George Mason ducked under the porch, where he thought he'd be hidden, at least for a while. Mom found him.

"Come on out, boy! You could have hurt your brother. Why did you do that?"

He stayed under the porch and refused to come out. He probably thought, "Maybe, just, maybe, they will forget about me," and the spanking he knew awaited him.

Once Dad got home from work and heard the story, he tried coaxing George Mason. He still wouldn't budge. Dad told Mom, "Let him stay. When it gets dark, he'll be happy to come from under that porch."

As Dad predicted, George Mason's fear of a spanking was no match for the darkness. As the sun set, with few, if any, streetlights near the house, his fear of the dark got the best of him. Finally, he crawled from under the porch and went into the house.

"Couldn't take the dark any longer, huh?" Dad remarked as he reached for the switch lying on the table in front of him. Before the switch touched George Mason's legs, the tears began rolling down his face.

"Boy, I bet you'll think twice before you do anything like that again," Dad said.

The spanking he tried to avoid was waiting for him and no less stinging than if he had received it hours before. As he lay on the bed trying to recover from the painful episode, he had no idea just how much things would continue to change.

George Mason began attending nursery school, where he was not the center of attention and learned how to share. Each weekday, he anxiously awaited to be picked up by someone from Mother Goose Nursery School.

"Mama, the people from Mother Goose are here!" he would call out as he stood at the door, watching for the car to pull up in front of the house.

George Mason is with his Mother Goose Nursery School classmates and teachers in 1947. Mrs. Nickerson stands on the left in the rear. George Mason is in the last row, the fourth child from the right.

Thelma Nickerson, the school's owner and the operator was a neighbor of ours. In the early days of the school, classes were held at someone's home. She would later move the school to the basement of Second Baptist, an African American church about twenty minutes from our neighborhood. In nursery school, everyone learned the alphabet, numbers, colors, and social skills. When you left Mother Goose, you were ready for first grade.

Before the end of the year, Mom and Dad found and purchased the home they so desperately wanted. Dad's status as a veteran made a big difference in securing a loan to buy the property through the VA Home Loan Guaranty program. The program started in 1944 to help veterans returning from the war buy a home.

In November, Mom, Dad, George Mason, and Mike moved to 1909 North Dinwiddie Street. There was so much to be thankful for. A new home, two healthy boys, and another baby on the way. On November 17, 1947, Mom and Dad would celebrate their sixth wedding anniversary. They were filled with gratitude to see how far they had come.

Their new house was only about ten minutes away from Nana's, and closer to Grandma Jones' home, which sat one street over from Dinwiddie. You could cut through the neighbor's driveway across the street and be in Grandma Jones' backyard in a flash. Most people didn't have a fence around their yard back then, and people were neighborly. They didn't mind you taking a shortcut through their driveway or backyard occasionally.

There were family members all around.

Two doors up from Mom and Dad's new home was the house Dad's great-grandmother Elizabeth had purchased after she settled in Arlington as a free woman. Since she died in 1931, her stepdaughter, Ida, and her son, Earl, remained there. Uncle Earl—that's what we called him—was our Dad's cousin. Growing up, we would stop by to visit Uncle Earl and his wife, whom we called Aunt Teenie. We always made sure we grabbed a few grapes from their idyllic looking grape orchard in the backyard.

Mom and Dad's house didn't have a grape orchard, but it had a big backyard. It was a cute, red brick house with green shutters that framed the two front windows and a small porch that led to the front door. It wasn't a porch like Nana's. It was just big enough for a couple of people to step up on before entering the house.

In their living room and on the first floor, there were beautiful hardwood floors. The living room had a wood-burning fireplace with a classic mantle that framed it at the far end of the living room. Many years later, my siblings and I would rush from our beds to sit in front of the fireplace before school on cold winter mornings.

When they bought the house, only the first floor was complete. The house had an unfinished basement and attic, which gave them room to expand. Mom and Dad wasted no time, adding two bedrooms in the attic area. By the time they moved in, they had four bedrooms.

The additional bedrooms gave them space to grow, but the house still only had one small bathroom. For a family of three—soon to be four—that wasn't a big issue. The bathroom was big enough for a bathtub and shower combo, a small sink, and a toilet—nothing fancy, just the necessities and enough room for a small stool. The bathroom, like the kitchen, had a nice window with a great view of the backyard. Mom would find that the view from the kitchen window was perfect for keeping her eye on all of us as we played out back in years to come.

Now Mom had a house, like her closest friends. Mom had been friends with Patience, whom we called Aunt Pat, and her sister, Rosa, since they were kids. Our families were very close, making Aunt Pat and her husband, Uncle Alonzo, great godparents for Mike. Mom and Dad would later become godparents too.

Idabel and George Jones were on their way. In a few months, they would bring baby number three into their home on Dinwiddie Street. In years to come, it would be pretty typical for any of us, except George Mason, to meet someone who knew an older brother or sister, to say, "You must be a Jones."

The home our parents bought at 1909 N. Dinwiddie Street.

CHAPTER 6

Be Fruitful and Multiply

Mom and Dad were not alone. Young couples across America were buying homes, having kids, and beginning life in a world at peace. Many years later, children born after World War II would be responsible for one of the largest birth rate increases and the most prolonged period of sustained fertility in the country. In the Jones household, six of the seven children they would bring into the world would be part of the baby boom generation.[8]

The second Jones to join the post-war baby boom was Rosalind, born on February 16, 1948. Mom's other best friend, Rosa, whom we called Aunt Roro, became her godmother. She was born thirteen months after Mike, who didn't seem ready to cede his place as the baby. Mike had yet to start walking.

8 U.S. Department of Commerce, U.S. Census Bureau, *The Baby Boom Cohort in the United States: 2012 to 2060*, by Sandra L. Colby and Jennifer M. Ortman, P25-141, (Washington, D.C., 2014).

Mother Goose had prepared George Mason for elementary school and helped him become a little less selfish with his brother and sister. Now that he was a first grader at Langston Elementary School, he had schoolwork and other interests to occupy him.

As a small and close-knit community, it wasn't surprising that families and kids worshipped, played, and were educated together.

Our family spent a lot of time with Aunt Pat, Aunt Roro, and their families. Mom and her two best friends grew up at Mount Salvation. All three were very active members of the Usher Board and the senior choir, and they attended and worked with the Sunday School. They were like the Three Musketeers. If you saw Aunt Pat and Aunt RoRo, Mom was usually with them too.

Mom was in all those groups, but she had a deep commitment to Sunday School. She believed in the scripture "Train up a child in the way he should go, and when he is old, he will not depart from it." That's how Mom and Dad's parents raised them and their brothers and sisters. Mom was a real student of the Bible, dedicating time daily to reading and studying the scriptures.[9]

Bible study prepared her for the leadership roles she would eventually assume as Sunday School assistant superintendent and later, superintendent. Roz recalls Mom saying, "I wanted to become a teacher." Her work as a Sunday School teacher and later as a leader seemed like the perfect way to fulfill her desire to teach. Our mother's day-to-day activities were centered around creating a wholesome life for our family with faith and service to God at the core.

---

9 Proverbs 6:22, (King James Version).

At church, Roz and Mike stayed with Mom since they were still toddlers. George Mason was old enough to attend the primary Sunday School class. In our house, honoring God didn't end with attending church. We attended Sunday School, followed by morning service, and frequently were in late afternoon or evening services. Even if there were no evening or afternoon services, we could not participate in activities not associated with the church.

Even though Mom was married with several children, Nana continued to influence her life strongly. Nana had a strict view on the sabbath, and if the focus did not include honoring God, you shouldn't be doing it. She had no qualms sharing her displeasure with Mom if she allowed us to do something for which she did not approve.

I can imagine Nana saying something like this: "Idabel, you aren't letting those children go to the movies on Sunday, are you?"

The Bible said, on the seventh day, God rested. As Christians, Nana expected us to strictly follow the sentiment of the scriptures. Mom adhered to that rule until Nana passed.

Fortunately, Sunday School offered fun activities for kids and families. George Mason especially looked forward to the Sunday School beach outing, and in the future, we would all agree with him.

The beach trip on July 28, 1951, became almost legendary in our family. It was the day of the Sunday School annual trip to Carr's and Sparrow's Beach in Annapolis, Maryland. A few years later, Fort Smallwood in Anne Arundel County, Maryland, would replace Carr's and Sparrows' Beach. There were less than a handful of public beaches open to Black people close enough for a day trip. Beaches, like everything else, were segregated.

George Mason was nine years old at the time. The beach trip was his once-a-year opportunity to play in the Chesapeake Bay and in the sand. Mike was four, and Roz was three. At the beach, the grownups would hang out under the shelter, talking, and enjoying the day, as they kept their eyes on the kids. It was a day for the whole family to relax, enjoy the outdoors, and consume lots of good food.

Preparing enough food to last a family of five for six hours at the beach fell to Mom. She spent the entire day before the outing in the kitchen, but it started a few days before then with the list.

Mom and Dad would gather in the kitchen to decide what was needed, and Dad wrote everything down.

"Let's see, George. Do you have the list?" Mom would say.

"Go ahead, Idabel. I'm ready," said Dad.

"Okay, we need grapes, soft drinks, and potato chips. And get mayonnaise and a dozen eggs."

That's the way it was. Mom told Dad what to put on the list, and Dad did the grocery shopping. Mom cooked fried chicken, made potato salad, and deviled eggs. In the cooler, she placed grapes, plums, and soft drinks. And she packed potato chips, paper plates, and all the other fixings for the trip.

Mom made sure the beach towels were packed—although they probably were just regular bath towels we took to the beach. She packed the kids bathing suits and chose clothes for Mike and Roz. As always, she made sure everything was done, despite this time being nine months pregnant.

Mom and Dad packed and organized everything, and everyone went to bed. They would have an early morning start for the three-hour drive to the beach. In the morning, the families would gather in their cars in the church parking lot and depart together.

The next morning, their plans went south when Mom went into labor.

Mom anxiously woke Dad. "George, I think the baby is coming."

"Now?" Dad said.

Mom said George Mason was really upset when he found out it was time for her to have the baby. Years later, she would laugh, recalling how out of sorts George Mason was that day. "All George Mason could think about was that the baby was messing up his trip to the beach!"

In those days and especially as our family grew, a trip to the beach was the closest the Jones kids got to a family vacation. I imagine the beach was probably the highlight of George Mason's summer. Just the thought of losing out had him pouting.

Dad made it clear: "George Mason, the baby is coming, and there is nothing we can do about that."

They marshaled all of the family resources. Mom called Nana and asked her to go with her to the hospital. Grandma Jones or another family member would watch George Mason, Mike, and Roz, while Dad took Mom to deliver the baby. They must have been a little nervous. Although I can't imagine their mannerisms or words showed any evidence of worry. They were not the kind of people to show stress.

Dad had a lot to balance. He had to get Mom to the hospital safely, which was no small feat. If he could have taken her around the corner to Arlington Hospital, it would have been so much easier. Mom couldn't have her baby there. They wouldn't admit Black women to the maternity ward.[10]

They picked up Nana and made the forty-minute drive to Freedman's Hospital in DC. Dad made sure Mom was admitted and then headed back to Arlington to pick up Roz, Mike, and George Mason. When Dad arrived back home from the hospital, he packed the car with all the food Mom had prepared for the outing. Roz, Mike, and George Mason jumped into the car, and off to the beach they went.

As the beach trip came to an end, Dad must have been exhausted. He started his morning with a trip to Freedman's Hospital, followed by a three-hour drive each way to the beach. But his day wasn't over. After he got the kids back to Hall's Hill, he took them to Grandma Jones' house. Then he went back to DC to see how Mom and the new baby were doing.

Dad didn't know, but the real excitement was only beginning. When he arrived at the nursery, he received a lovely but surprising sight. There were two Jones babies. It had been quite a day. It started with three kids, and in less than a few hours, he had five. Mom and Dad had a set of twins, a boy and a girl.

In 1951, there were no sonograms, so it was impossible to know the sex of the fetus or if a woman was carrying more than one baby. When my sister, Wilma, interviewed Dad for a book she was writing about Hall's Hill, she asked him what his reaction was upon seeing he had two babies. Our dad was a very practical man, and his response to Wilma was reflective of George Jones through and through. He told

10 Les Shaver, "Crossing the Divide," *Arlington Magazine*, October 15, 2013.

her that all he could think was, "We need a second crib and a whole lot more diapers."

The newest Joneses were my brother Lynwood and me. Lynwood was born five minutes before me. Down to the last minute, even the doctor thought Mom was only carrying one baby. As soon as he delivered Lynwood, Mom thought there was something odd. She told the doctor, "I still feel something." She was right. What she felt was me. They now had four kids under five years old.

In the days and weeks to come, Mom and Dad would often look to their mothers to help babysit their expanded family. Raising four kids under five years old would be challenging for anyone, so an extra hand or two gave Mom a breather.

Mom brought Lynwood and me home from the hospital about five days later—a typical length of stay in the 1950s. Since it was summertime, George Mason wasn't in school. I can't be sure, but Mike, Roz, and George Mason probably stayed with Grandma Jones until Mom came home from the hospital. Her house was very close, and it would be easy for Dad to check on them before work and when he got home. I imagine George Mason spent a lot of time on the playground. It was so close to Grandma Jones' and Mom and Dad's house.

Once Lynwood and I were born, George Mason, Mike, and Roz spent more time with Nana and Grandma Jones. She was handling two newborn babies, two toddlers, and a nine year old, which left Mom little time for anything else. She might have time to catch up on her household chores or sit down for a minute or two by occasionally sending the three older children to their grandmothers.

Nana's house was like a second home, especially for George Mason and Mike. George Mason had friends who lived near Nana's. It had been his home until he was six years old. Both boys spent hours playing outside. They ran back and forth between Nana's house and Ms. Edgie and Mr. Sam Harrington, her good friends and neighbors. Mike and George Mason had great fun playing with the neighborhood kids who Mike referred to as "the 22nd Street gang" and eating fruit from the Harrington's many trees.

Mike had some very special memories about time he spent learning how to read while visiting the Harrington's home.

"I spent a lot of time playing outside and going over Ms. Edgie's and Mr. Sam Harrington's. I used to take the comic strips from Sunday paper to their house and lay on the floor. I would spread the paper out and read the comics. They helped me with the words I didn't know, and they helped me read. This was before I started school."

Roz was three and spent more time in the house with Nana. But whenever she had to go to the bathroom, she had to use the outhouse. Roz hated the large spiders sometimes crawling around in there. When Uncle Clarence built a bathroom inside the house, she was one happy little girl.

Summertime always seemed to be busy for the Jones family, but few could come close to the summer of 1951. A month after Lynwood and I were born, George Mason returned to Langston and began the fourth grade. Langston Elementary opened its doors in 1925. Mom, Dad, and now George Mason attended elementary school there. Mike started at Mother Goose Nursery School in the fall. Roz was still home with Mom, me, and Lynwood.

Before Mike started nursery school, he was already reading. He didn't need to learn his ABCs, and Mrs. Nickerson recognized he was more advanced than the average nursery school student. She felt Mike had the skills to succeed in first grade and suggested that Mom and Dad have him tested for early admission. Mike performed well on the test, and at the start of the next school year, in 1952, he entered first grade at five years old.

Once Mom had more kids, she hired a neighbor to babysit Roz, Lynwood, and me. One year later, in the fall of 1953, Roz began attending preschool at Mother Goose when she was five. Mike was six and moving on to the second grade, and George Mason was a sixth grader and in his last year at Langston.

A month after everyone went back to school, another baby girl arrived on October 17, 1953. Mom and Dad named her Audrey. With six children, Mom took a job working closer to home in the cafeteria at Langston. The neighbor continued to watch Audrey, Lynwood, and me while Mom worked. The hours at the new job would be better for managing their growing family. Mom could get everyone off for school and return home before school was out.

There had been many memorable moments for our family since moving into the new home. 1909 N Dinwiddie went from a fairly quiet household to one bustling with energy. Five years later, they had six kids, and one soon to be a teenager.

Things were looking up at Dad's job as well. The machinist program he had been interested in before going off to the army was still active. Dad had reapplied to the program. This time the outcome was positive. Once again, Dad's veteran status opened the door to opportunities. Having served in World War II, he was eligible for government programs that gave veterans preferential standing.

Mom and Dad did not believe in giving up. Dad's tenacity was paying off and opening doors to help increase his income and better provide for our large family.

CHAPTER 7

Langston Elementary School

Despite legal battles, Arlington's Black communities continued to fight to desegregate schools and gain better resources. By the time George Mason entered junior high school, there was still little to show for their efforts. The state of Virginia justified their segregation policies by labeling them as separate but equal. They were separate...yet far from equal.

George Mason entered seventh grade at Hoffman Boston Junior-Senior High School in the fall of 1954. In our community, it was simply H-B. If you were Black and lived in Arlington, in the 1950s, you went to H-B from seventh through twelfth grades. Some parents chose to have their children stay with a relative in DC, where Black people could attend several schools, and more advanced courses were available.

Hall's Hill kids didn't have a neighborhood junior or senior high school or even one within walking distance.

George Mason and all the Hall's Hill students rode the school bus. From our neighborhood, the ride took about thirty-five minutes. The bus drove past the whites-only Washington-Lee High School area, only fifteen minutes after departing Hall's Hill. For Black students attending senior high school in Arlington, their trip to H-B on Johnson's Hill would continue for an additional twenty minutes.

When they finally arrived at H-B, the doors to the bus opened, and the students filed out, bidding farewell to the driver. They entered the small building, each student dressed in the latest styles. The girls were sporting the cute hairstyles, wide skirts, and an armful of books. The boys were directly behind them wearing their collared-shirts, button-up sweaters, and skinny-leg slacks, also carrying an armful of books.

Academics didn't diminish their interest in the latest fashion trends, hairstyles, sports, and parties.

George Mason was growing up and looking more like Dad every day. His facial features and complexion were both like Dad's: beautiful chocolate skin and a sharp nose. He had a great personality and a smile to match. His slim, athletic build was a perfect attribute for the baseball and basketball teams. By the time he graduated from high school, he would be close to six feet tall and one of the team's better players.

Practice sessions for sports teams typically held after school created transportation challenges for Hall's Hill students. "Robert and I were the boys from 'the Hill' who played sports. Sometimes the games or practices ran long, so we had to walk home from Johnson's Hill if we missed the bus. If it was cold, we caught the public bus going to Walker

Chapel. We got off on Glebe Road and Lee Highway and walked another ten minutes to our neighborhood," George Mason recalled.

On the days when the weather was decent, George Mason and Robert's walk from Johnson's Hill to Hall's Hill took about ninety minutes.

Like most teenagers, George Mason couldn't wait to leave the watchful eye of neighbors and teachers who knew Mom and Dad very well. Attending H-B was his chance to gain a degree of independence. And with that independence, Mom and Dad expected more responsibility. For himself and others, the allure of social life, football games, dating, and parties was what they yearned for.

When George Mason and his classmates entered H-B—all at once—their social circle changed. There were students from Johnson's Hill and Green Valley, the other African American community in South Arlington. H-B was one of the few chances they had to meet. For George Mason, it would be the first of many opportunities to expand beyond the bounds of Hall's Hill.

Sports were important for students, but it didn't take precedence over academics. And a great deal of their success was a testament to the school's great teachers. The "separate but equal" resources Virginia touted left a lot to be desired.

Mr. George Richardson was the principal at H-B from 1951 until its closing in 1964. When he spoke to an Oklahoma oral history group about the inadequate resources during his tenure, his opinions remained visceral. Hoffman-Boston "wasn't equipped as well as other schools. Our science department wasn't equipped well. Other departments were not. We didn't have an auditorium—the building wasn't adequate."[11]

In contrast, he fondly recalled the students and faculty at a 2010 student reunion. "We had an excellent group of students…And I think we had the best staff, truly."[12]

From their personal funds and time, Black teachers supplemented the resources provided by the Arlington County School system. They had a deep connection to the neighborhoods, the students, and their families. It was an investment in the future of the Black community. *The next doctor. The next teacher.* They would never know who might be the next George Washington Carver, W.E.B. DuBois, Frederick Douglass, or Mary McLeod Bethune if they didn't invest in their learning.

That wasn't only the case at Hoffman-Boston; it was true of teachers at Langston Elementary as well.

In the Jones household, 1954 didn't just usher in new school experiences for George Mason; it was an exciting year for Roz too. Early in her youth, school and teaching had captured Roz's imagination.

"I liked school. I started playing school at home with you, Lynwood, and Audrey when I was pretty young." From the start, Roz was anxious to learn new things and absorb everything Langston had to offer.

Roz didn't experience the angst many students had on the first day of school. Langston was a neighborhood school. As she entered the first-grade classroom, looking around

11 Scott McCaffrey, "Principal of Arlington's Segregated Black High School Dies at 102," *Inside NOVA*, June 19, 2015.

12 Ibid.

the room, Roz spotted one familiar face after another. They attended Mount Salvation Baptist Church, or Mrs. Nickerson's preschool, or spent time on the playground. One nursery school friend she saw was Sheila Brown. They became buddies at Langston and would go on to be lifelong friends.

Langston Elementary had a multidimensional role in our community. In many ways, the school and the all-Black fire station across the street from Langston, Fire Station Number 8, were the hubs of our community fulfilling multiple purposes beyond their designated function.

The year before Roz began attending school, Langston expanded beyond the original red brick, four-classroom building. They had a cafeteria that doubled as a multipurpose room and first and second-grade classrooms near the new school office on the first floor. The expansion of Langston meant Fire Station 8 was no longer the only place civic groups and organizations could meet.

The John M. Langston Citizens Association, a powerful community organization, moved their meetings to Langston's multipurpose room. And, groups later organized like the Boy Scouts and Brownie troops met at the Firehouse.

For a few hours during the day, the multipurpose room became a lunchroom. Mr. Mervin, the school janitor who was a close family friend, would unfold the long tables and benches that had been recessed into the wall and locked in place. They were reminiscent of a Murphy bed. At the end of the lunch period, he cleaned them off and placed them back into the wall. After school, the room became a rehearsal and practice area for cultural and fine arts activities offered through the recreation department.

A copy of Langston Elementary School's dedication program commemorating its new cafeteria, multipurpose room, office, and two classrooms.

In those days, segregation touched every aspect of life, even Arlington's recreation department. An African American man named Mr. Johnson managed the recreation department for Arlington's Black communities. There were a variety of activities to choose from. Students paid a fee for all kinds of lessons: piano, tap dance, ballet, majorette, saxophone, and clarinet. Most of the kids in our family took lessons after school. I took tap dance, and Roz took majorettes.

Walking past the multipurpose room after school, you would hear light and joyful sounds. *Click, click. Click, click.* You heard the tapping of metal from the shiny patent shoes as they connected with the linoleum floors. On an alternate day, you would hear the cadence of one-to-three, one-to-three, as the ballet teacher called out the moves.

Just beyond the multipurpose room in the library, students took piano, clarinet, and saxophone lessons. You didn't only hear the sounds and expressions of happiness coming from the multipurpose room and the library—you could feel them.

The biggest beneficiaries of Langston's expanded facility were the teachers and students. The addition of the kitchen and multipurpose room meant students could eat lunch at school. Whether your lunch was from the cafeteria, where Mom worked, or a brown bag, students now had a designated space to eat.

Having Mom close by during school was usually a plus, except when one of our teachers informed her that our behavior wasn't up to standards. Roz remembers her unfortunate lunchtime encounters: "Mom used to give me a hard time at lunch if I talked too much in class, and the teacher let her know."

None of us would be exempt from Mom's stern look or reprimand during school as time went on.

As we got older, Dad and Mom sometimes needed Roz and Mike to take on additional responsibilities for short periods, especially with Nana and Grandma Jones. Both of our grandmothers began experiencing more health issues and were less able to do everything independently.

When Mike was in fifth and sixth grade, Dad asked him to help out with Grandma Jones. For a while, he moved in with her and spent the night at her house. It was an experience he fondly remembers.

"I used to come home from school and go over to her house. I slept on the sofa in the dining room area at Grandma Jones' for about two years. I had a great time with her. She had the littlest cast iron frying pan, and she would prepare scrambled eggs for me in that pan. She was a very sweet lady, and it was a very nice experience. I really enjoyed it."

Mom asked Roz to help out in a similar way when she was in the fifth and sixth grades. During the week, she would go to Nana's house to warm up her dinner, and at Mom's insistence, Mike had to go along. Roz recalls Mike being more of a "nuisance" than any help.

He would walk a few steps behind Roz. Out of the blue, she would feel pebbles hitting her. She'd turn around and catch him in the act of throwing stones at her. Mike didn't want to be there. He preferred to be on the playground with his friends or reading a book. He didn't see why Mom wanted him to tag along with Roz, and neither did she. Mike's stone-throwing never caused Roz any pain; he was just a knucklehead.

Lynwood and I wouldn't arrive at Langston until 1957. Mom had worked at the school long enough to be a part of the Langston culture. When you thought about Langston, you also thought about Mom or Ms. Idabel as all the kids in the community referred to her as. She, Mrs. Hazel, and Eunice were the "lunch ladies." They worked as a team in the Langston cafeteria. Mr. Mervin didn't work in the kitchen, but he was a part of their team.

School lunches in the 1950s were almost like dinner. We had a variety of vegetables, always, from a can. Everyone ate canned food in the fifties. The previously frozen chopped meat disguised as beef, and we sometimes had fish sticks. As long as the taste was good, it didn't matter to us. Occasionally, we had canned spaghetti or frozen pizza, probably Chef Boyardee. All the Jones kids bought lunch at school. The downside of buying lunch at Langston for us was returning the tray. With Mom in the cafeteria, we had to eat all of our food. If our plates were not clean, she would send us back to eat *everything*. Those rules weren't just for me, Lynwood, and Roz; it went for other kids too.

At the time, I didn't understand why she made such a fuss, but looking back, I realize just how tough things were for both of my parents growing up. Between living through the Great Depression, growing up with only one parent to carry the load, and not being paid a fair wage because of their race, waste was not in their vocabulary.

Mom gave anyone who attempted to turn their tray in with uneaten food on it a hard way to go. I have a vivid memory of one classmate who didn't like lima beans. Every time we had lima beans for lunch, he wouldn't eat them, and when he attempted to return his tray, he was reprimanded.

At that time, when we returned our trays with the plates and silverware—no plastic spoons or forks back then—we had to physically turn them into one of the "lunchroom ladies." And, when it was Mom who took your tray, hopefully, your plate was clean. For one of our classmates, lima bean day was never a good day.

When Lynwood and I arrived at Langston, we did our best to follow the rules, especially during lunch. The last thing we wanted was a reprimand from the teacher and Mom.

In first and second grade, we had the benefit of being in the same classroom. Even if we hadn't known anyone else, we had each other. Between nursery school, church, and family friendships, our school friends were almost like our extended family. Jimmy was Mrs. Hazel's son. She worked with Mom in the cafeteria, and Marguarite was Eunice's niece, also a lunch lady. Curtis was Aunt Pat's son, and we had been at school and church together since we were toddlers. Charlene went to Sunday School with us. So did Jimmy.

Between school and church, we might see each other six days a week. From first grade to sixth grade, Saturday was likely the only day we were not in each other's company.

Roz was now in the fourth grade, and Mike was a sixth grader. The following year, Mike would attend H-B with George Mason, who was busy making a name for himself as an athlete. Rosalind and Sheila's friendship had grown stronger. Each year they had been in the same classroom. Their love for school is likely one of the things that drew them to each other.

We were connected to our classmates through close friendships or our sense of community, sometimes both. Our teachers filled the gap between the history books and African Americans' contributions to America's history. They taught us about our place in history and made sure we knew who contributed and how.

Teachers, parents, and community leaders banded together. They worked through the school and citizen's association to secure equal treatment and equal rights for which generations of Black Americans had already toiled, fought, and died.

The John M. Langston Citizens Association had been advocating for equal treatment in the allocation of county resources since its creation in 1924. Black folks could not afford to sit back and be silent. If you didn't speak up, there was no chance we would be treated equally by the county.

Families with children at Langston and H-B had been working with NAACP attorneys for years to force Arlington County to integrate the school system. Our parents joined with neighbors and the greater community to fight for the rights we deserved.

Unsurprisingly, many of the same people who worked to improve educational opportunities and enhance our quality of life were also involved in the faith community and fighting for equal rights. The work was never-ending, and the hours they spent together created bonds and relationships among parents and their children.

Between Langston, our churches, the playground, and our extracurricular activities, my brothers, sisters, and I enjoyed the advantages gained from our parent's tenacious fight to give us a better life. It was all invisible to us at the time, but it was purposeful and planned. Our generation and those following us would benefit from their efforts and be a part of revolutionary change for our families.

CHAPTER 8

Summertime

As kids, many of our most unforgettable moments happened in the three months between the last day of school and Labor Day. Summer brought with it an air of freedom. The day school ended, everything suddenly slowed down, and it felt like we didn't have a care in the world.

In 1958, Lynwood and I had just finished first grade, and we could go to the playground on our own—or at least with Roz. We explored the neighborhood, especially the wooded areas and creeks nearby. It wasn't as rural as when our parents grew up, but there were still wooded areas that beckoned to us to come in and explore.

But our adventures almost always started on the playground.

Somehow, everything worth remembering seemed squeezed into June, July, and August. We played and worshipped. Our friendships grew. Even teenagers, who had part-time jobs and didn't have the luxury of total freedom, found time to hang out with friends at the beach and enjoy a lawn party, just as our parents had done.

It was all at once an ordinary and memorable, carefree, and magical time.

I was always an early morning riser, especially in the summertime. If the sun was up, I was too—even at six or seven years old. In the steamy, hot summer days, we cooled our upstairs bedroom with screens placed in the windows. Nearly every morning, I heard a woodpecker hammering on a tree. There was a chorus of nature sounds with the next-door neighbor's rooster chiming in for a while.

I'd sit up, look out the window, hoping to see the woodpecker. It seemed so close. But I never laid my eyes on that bird. When I looked back at Roz and Audrey, they were still sleeping. Getting out of bed, I was careful not to wake them. Then I walked down the hall past Mike and Lynwood's bedroom and downstairs to the bathroom.

In our house, getting up at dawn wasn't about the early bird catching the worm; it was getting into the bathroom and out before my brothers and sisters woke up. With only one toilet in the house, our timing was everything. Some days, I wouldn't be so lucky.

When I hit the bottom step and saw the bathroom door closed, I'd sigh. Darn.

Sitting on the steps where I could see the door, I waited until it started to open. Not a chance anyone wouldn't know I was next.

But more often than not, when I came down the stairs, I could hear Mom in the kitchen, water running, cabinet doors closing. I peeked into the kitchen and greeted her as if I'd been up for hours.

"Good morning, Mama."

"Good morning, Lydia. Did you have a good night's sleep?"

"Yes, ma'am." And into the bathroom I would go. It only took a minute for someone to slip by and get ahead of me.

Occasionally, I awoke even earlier. Mom might still be sitting in her chair in the living room, reading her Bible. She always began her day with prayer and a private moment of worship.

On the weekdays, we headed straight to the playground. Once Mom gave the okay, we were gone. Saturdays were different. Dad and Mom had a routine that started with creating the week's grocery list.

"George, we're out milk. We probably need a gallon to hold us over until the milkman comes next week. You know Mike can drink a gallon by himself," Mom would say.

"Anything else?" said Dad.

"Pick up roast beef for dinner tomorrow, chicken, liver, and fish sticks for later in the week."

They would go on and on until Dad had created the shopping list of all the items Mom wanted him to buy.

Then, Dad would let us know he was leaving.

"Hey, Rozzie, Lynwood, and Lydia; come on, we're going to the Safeway." When Audrey was older, she'd come along too.

We'd yell out, "Here we come, Daddy."

Through the kitchen and out the back door, we'd run, jumping into Dad's black Plymouth. Before going to the Safeway, we stopped at Nana's to pick up Uncle Dede. He would shop for himself and Nana at the same time Dad was buying groceries for our family. From Nana's, it was a short trip up Lee Highway to the grocery store. Most businesses of note were on Lee Highway. It's where Langston Elementary School and Fire Station 8 were too. Closer to our neighborhood were several Black-owned businesses, two barbershops, the dentist office, and me and Lynwood's godmother Adeles' Beauty Salon. Further down were the Safeway and People's Drug Store.

On the way to the grocery store, I thought about the allowance Dad would give us and what I wanted to buy. Dad parked in the Safeway lot and gave us each twenty-five cents allowance to spend on whatever we wanted. Across the street to the five- and ten-cent store we ran, and Dad went grocery shopping.

We entered the store, almost bouncing in anticipation of what toy we might choose. Up and down the aisles, we walked until some toy or item caught our eye. Before long, we would feel the glare of a middle-aged white lady with black hair staring us down. My natural inclination was to smile and say hi, but her glare was cold and grimacing. Instead, my shoulders tensed, my head slightly dropped, in one moment shrinking as if to hide, and in the next feeling afraid. Her scowl and mean spirit made us feel unwelcome. She didn't need to speak with disdain. She wanted us to *feel* like we didn't belong.

As we got older, we became more determined and stopped recoiling. We let go of our fear. With our heads held high, we continued to shop there whenever we wanted. The woman in the five- and ten-cent store never watched or followed the white kids that came in, and we noticed. Every time we went in, she followed us. Those weekly visits to the five- and ten-cent store were our first one-on-one encounters with racism.

When we met Dad and Uncle Dede back at the Safeway, we'd jump in his car and drive down Lee Highway back towards Hall's Hill to Nana's house. We learned to leave those racist encounters back in the store. Our parents helped us understand that it was her problem and not worth our time. It was just the way white people were. Their loss; it wasn't worth taking up space in our head.

Turning off 22nd Street onto Frederick Street, we neared the long unpaved driveway leading up to our grandmother's back door. Dad opened the trunk, revealing lots of grocery bags. He and Dede grabbed the groceries for Nana's house from the car, and we ran into the house to see Nana.

Our faces lit up, and our eyes sparkled as we rushed to hug Nana. Most often, she was sitting in a small alcove between the kitchen and the dining room. Next to her was a quaint marble-top antique side table where her beautiful African Violet plants sat. They were healthy and vibrant, showcasing her green thumb.

Dad and Dede unloaded the groceries, and we would sit and talk to Nana. After dispensing with hugs, she looked at our knees and elbows for ash, cuts, and scratches.

"Let me see those knees," she would say to us. "Now, the elbows. Roz, get me that lemon cream from the shelf."

If our knees were a little ashy or getting dark from playing on them in the yard, she would rub them with a lemony cream. Now and then, we would get a dose of that cream applied to the back of our necks too. I can't say I looked forward to having my knees, elbows, and the backside of my neck rubbed with lemon cream, but it wasn't painful, and I especially liked the smell.

We loved spending time with her, and all the girls were fascinated by her hair. It was beautiful. One thing we were not allowed to do was comb her hair. One day, Audrey gave it a try.

"I asked her if I could comb her hair. At first, she said yes. But I don't think she heard me clearly, because when I started touching her hair, she said, 'No.'"

Nana had high cheekbones, sharp features, and thin lips. Our mother and her siblings had the same features. But no one's hair was as beautiful as our grandmother's.

After a short visit and dropping off the groceries, we left for home. Mom was there waiting for us as we pulled up in the driveway. Everyone grabbed a bag, entered through the back door to the kitchen, placing each bag on the table.

"Once you get everything in the house, unload the bags and put the food away, girls," Mom would say.

We returned to the car to get more bags until the trunk was empty.

"When you finish, get something to eat, and then you can go out to play."

Like every other summer day, Mike was always on the playground, even on the weekends. The recreation department didn't offer weekend organized activities, so the rest of us played in the backyard. Our big oak tree was perfect for climbing. We had a sandbox and plenty of grassy space to play baseball. We almost had enough people for a baseball team, but many neighborhood kids would also come over.

The only rules: stay clear of Mom's clothesline, and don't break the basement window. Much too often, a baseball ended up in the window. Once we broke it, Dad would be pretty angry with us. He didn't bother replacing the glass until the end of every summer. He knew it would likely be a waste of time, so he placed a cut piece of plywood in the window, and then repaired it in the fall before the start of school.

Almost every Saturday afternoon, Dad and some of his Hall's Hill friends drove to the horse races in Charles Town, West Virginia. He enjoyed the racetrack and betting on horse races. Like Dad caddying on Sundays, his enjoyment of horse racing wasn't something Mom cared for. Although, she knew Dad would never let the racetrack create any risks for our family. One afternoon, when I was much older, Dad didn't have anyone to ride to Charles Town with him. The racetrack was in the West Virginia mountains and not a drive anyone wanted to take alone, especially at night. They drove up at dusk. On the way home, it would be very dark.

"Hey, Lydia, do you want to drive up to Charles Town with me?"

I thought, wow, Dad wants me to go to the track with him. "Yeah Dad, I'd love to go with you."

And off we went! It was so cool to hang out with Dad by myself. I don't remember much about the drive up except that there were lots of hills and curves. We parked and went in.

"Do you want to place a bet?" he asked.

"Sure. But how do I do that?"

Dad gave me a couple of dollars and told me how the process worked. I picked my horse, and he placed my bet and his. The racetrack was different than any place I had been. The closest experience I had was going to a carnival. There were lots of people and lots of sounds. At the start of the race, the trumpet would play, the gate would open, and the yelling and cheering would ensue. We didn't stay too long, but it was fun. The best part was getting to spend time with just Dad.

On Saturday evenings, Aunt Pat and her kids, Jerry, Curtis, and Karen, would drive over, and she and Mom would sit out in the front yard, talk, and people watch. Sometimes an unsuspecting group of teenagers would walk past our house on their way to the playground and not notice Mom and Aunt Pat because it was dark. They never turned the porch light on while sitting outside. If someone were cursing or saying something off-color, Mom would call them on it. You would quickly hear, "I'm sorry, Miss Idabel." My mother didn't play. But everyone knew if you did something wrong in front of an adult, either they would call you on it or they would call your parents.

Mom and Aunt Pat would go right back to their conversation as if nothing happened. They could talk forever. We played hide and go seek until dusk arrived, then *blink, blink*—the lightning bugs were out. That was our cue to get some Mason jars from the kitchen and punch holes in the metal top. We didn't want to kill them before the night was over. Nothing was more fun than catching lightning bugs in the summertime. It didn't end too well for the lightning bugs, since they would soon die. But at that moment, it was the most fun.

Aunt Pat and Mom usually called it a night by nine-thirty or ten. School was out, and bedtimes were pretty relaxed, but we had church in the morning. We had to get in bed for an early start.

Sunday mornings, we could smell Dad cooking. Before seven, he was in the kitchen doing what he did every Sunday, cooking breakfast as Mom was busy getting ready for church.

It wasn't just the food that made Sunday morning breakfast special. Something about Dad taking the time to cook breakfast for us was just cool. I don't know what motivated him to cook on Sunday mornings. Maybe it was his way to give Mom a break from preparing meals every day, or maybe it was simply breakfast being something we all looked forward to.

Mom and Dad were a team. They worked together. Even though they grew up in the early part of the twentieth century, their marriage was more like a partnership. We didn't know any other dads who shopped for groceries and clothes and regularly cooked Sunday morning breakfast.

Dad had a routine. Get the sausage frying in one pan, and then start mixing the batter for his yummy pancakes. They weren't too big, and they weren't heavy and spongy like some pancakes can be. He used an off-the-shelf mix, but he would add wheat germ to them and cook them on his cast iron griddle. They were light with a crispy edge, finished off with a little butter. Sunday morning breakfast was always a treat. After he cooked, Dad would take a plate of pancakes over to Grandma Jones' house. I have rarely had a pancake anywhere as good as my father's.

Dad left to take Mom and the those of us who were younger to church around eight-thirty in the morning. As the Sunday School assistant superintendent, she had to arrive early to help with devotions. Roz and Mike could walk by themselves if they chose to, but they needed to be there by nine when Sunday School started.

When Dad arrived back home, he got ready for church or went to the country club to caddy. Whenever Dad chose a caddying job over going to church, it was a bone of contention for Mom. Years later, he would discontinue caddying on

Sunday, which ensured he could attend church every Sunday instead. On the days he readied for church, he had a few moments to enjoy the unusually quiet house. No children were running around. No conversation. It wasn't very often that there was so little activity at 1909 N Dinwiddie Street. Dad had the bathroom and the whole house to himself.

He took his suit from the closet and hung it on the door next to the shirt Mom had ironed for him. He set out his newly shined shoes, grabbed a pair of dark socks from the drawer, and then a tie, and put his handkerchief in his jacket pocket. Dad had excellent taste.

Then he took a leisurely bath and got ready for church in peace. By ten-thirty, Dad was driving up Dinwiddie Street. At the top of the hill, he would park near the rear of Calloway Methodist Church. The service didn't start until eleven, but Dad was an usher and hated to be late for anything.

At Mount Salvation Baptist, Audrey, Lynwood, and I were in the Sunday School primary class. We learned simple Bible verses and read Bible stories, and Roz and Mike were in the intermediate class. George Mason was rarely at Sunday School with us, but he would show up before church began. Dede was always at Sunday School too, but he rode to church with Mr. Clovis, who lived a block away from him on Frederick Street.

We went straight from Sunday School into the morning service at 11 a.m. Without exception, church service was long, particularly the preaching. The sermon was always pretty scary for a kid. Our minister, Reverend Richardson, might be described as a fire and brimstone preacher, but he was a kind man, and we were all fond of him. On a good day, the service ended by one in the afternoon.

The picture shows Mount Salvation Baptist Church in the 1950s.

When we got home, we would have an early Sunday dinner, which some people call supper.

Mom always cooked dinner on Saturday evenings. So, as soon as we arrived home from church, she turned on the oven to warm up the meal. While Mom changed out of her Sunday clothes, we set the table for dinner. Our dinners were pretty predictable, usually in a good way. Roast beef with gravy was always our meat for Sunday dinner. It never got boring. It was a treat. For us, it was like having a steak dinner once a week. We had plenty of vegetables, fresh greens, mashed potatoes, and maybe corn. Mom cooked a few chicken legs for herself. She wasn't much on roast beef, and Dad didn't particularly care for chicken.

We always ate Sunday dinner together when we were young. We sat at the kitchen table and said our blessing, talked, and enjoyed our meal and each other's company. Our kitchen was relatively small, so fitting eight people at the table meant there was little room to spare. We were kids, so we didn't give it a thought. Eating our Sunday meal together was fun, and the food was always delicious. It was our fanciest meal of the week. I was an excellent eater, and I earned the nickname "Chowhound" from my father. I wasn't offended. I knew he said it lovingly. It was all in fun. And I did love to eat. I was often the first at the table and almost always the last to leave.

On Sundays, we sometimes went back to church for afternoon service, much to our dismay. But there was an afternoon activity that we always looked forward to, a fund-raiser for one of the church auxiliaries held at Aunt Helen and Uncle Ernie's house in McLean, Virginia. They weren't related to us by blood, just in spirit. Over the years, it had become a tradition to hold this yearly fundraising event at their home.

Their house felt like a mansion, although we realized it was a modest-sized home when we were older. It was a two-bedroom house, with an attic and a basement—but it was well-appointed. As a kid, it was the surroundings that added to the grandeur of their home. They had a long gravel-lined driveway, a large front yard full of big beautiful trees, and a thick green lawn that looked like a carpet.

When we turned into the driveway, Audrey, Lynwood, and I focused on one thing. Gazing toward their large oak tree, we held our breath until we could see if anyone was already in the swing that hung from the tree at the front of their yard. No one wanted to wait for their chance at the swing. If it were empty, the competition would only be between the Jones kids to see who got to swing first.

Dad continued driving the car up the long driveway, past their white house with its long staircase leading to the front door. Lynwood, Audrey, Roz, and I were with Mom and Dad. Roz probably went with Mom to help out, but the rest of us jumped out of the car and ran toward the tree. When we got our chance, we would see how high we could fly. It felt amazing and freeing. It wasn't like the swings on the playground. It felt bigger and stronger, and we could fly so much higher in the air.

Aunt Pat and Uncle Alonzo brought Curtis, Jerry, and Karen. We all arrived early with other members of the church to help set up tables and chairs on the front lawn.

The property was beautiful and serene. The trees in the front yard seemed perfectly spaced, almost stately, and very tall. The lush leaf-filled tree limbs created a canopy that blocked all but streaks of sunlight, shading the tables and chairs. Many people from the church came, and a few brought their kids, but mostly it would be the Jones and the Spriggs kids and Reverend Richardson's daughter, Nathaline.

It was rare for a Black person to own that kind of property in McLean. In the 1950s, McLean was and continues to be an upper-class and more expensive area. I don't know how and when Uncle Ernie acquired their home and property, which extended beyond the house. On one side, there were acres of corn. That was farmland he worked riding his tractor and probably with workers he employed. On the other side, there were more crops growing and several acres of land. He rented that land out to some white farmers. Our visits to Uncle Ernie and Aunt Helen's home were always memorable. We went there for smaller get-togethers with Aunt Pat, Uncle Alonzo, Aunt RoRo, and a few other families from Mount Salvation.

Monday morning, Dad went back to his regular workday routine. That meant he was up and out of the house very early. Around six-thirty and no later than seven in the morning, he headed off to work at the Washington Navy Yard. Most of the time, he was gone before we were up. Mom's work schedule was the same as the school's, so she was off for the summer. Lynwood, Roz, and I knew we were going to the playground. Once Audrey was six or seven, she began to go with us too. George Mason had a summer job working at the Washington Golf and Country Club. Later on, he helped Mike get a job there. Even Dad worked at the Country Club to pick up some extra money on the weekends.

By nine, we were off, walking up Dinwiddie Street. We were at the shelter with the picnic tables at the playground's top-end in less than ten minutes. That's where we would find Jimmy's mom, Mrs. Hazel. She ran the summer program for the recreation department. Mrs. Hazel was a sweet lady, but she had her limits, and when she reached them, she laid down the law. Nearly all of the kids in our neighborhood were pretty good. Even the troublemakers would only go so far.

All the neighborhood kids met under the shelter for Mrs. Hazel to tell us what was planned for the day. We decided on what we wanted to do and then peeled off into groups. Until we got to fourth grade, Lynwood and I, and later Audrey, often spent time with Mrs. Hazel's group. We did arts and crafts, painting mimeographed pictures, making potholders with a hook-and-eye needle, and keychains from gimp string.

After our organized activities, it was pretty ad hoc—we played card games, checkers, chess, dominoes, Old Maid, or Jacks. After noontime, it got hot near the swings and the shelter. So, we would move down to an area on the other side of the baseball field. That was my favorite part of the playground. One beautiful grass-covered grove ran widthwise from Dinwiddie Street to the basketball court on the lower end of the play area. Trees dotted the space, interspersed between the picnic tables. The shade from the trees made it breezier than the area near the swings and covered shelter. It had a peaceful quality like you were in another world. It was easy to lose track of time.

Around noon, we went home to eat lunch. Mom didn't prepare lunch for us; it was self-service. She had worked nonstop, washing clothes, hanging them on the clothesline, and cleaning up the house. When we walked into the house, she was usually ironing clothes and watching one of her "stories," either *As the World Turns* or *All My Children* on television.

We headed to the bathroom to wash up and then looked in the refrigerator to see what we wanted for lunch. Usually, it was a peanut butter and jelly sandwich, a mayonnaise sandwich—which is just that—mayonnaise on two slices of bread, or hot dogs on white bread. We always had a lot of fruit in our house, so we might eat an apple, some grapes, or a banana. We stayed at home for about an hour, and then we went right back up the street.

In the evenings or when Mike finished cutting grass for neighbors, he played basketball or baseball. His love of basketball got him into trouble all the time. If there was a basketball game at the playground, Mike was there. When it got dark, he was supposed to come home, but he rarely did.

Mom would ask us when we came in for the evening, "Did you see Michael up there?"

"Yes, Mama, we saw him."

"Well, is he coming home?"

"He was still playing basketball when we left."

Mike talked about those times. "Mama was always telling me to come home and do this and do that. And I would tell her that I was in the middle of a game. When we finish the game, I'll come home."

That reasoning didn't work for Mom. She might go out into the front yard and yell Michael's name. We lived close enough that he could hear her. After a few minutes, if she didn't see him coming, she would start walking up the street to get him. Rarely did she make it all the way. It seemed like someone always alerted him. Some of us thought it might be Aunt Teenie, Uncle Earl's wife. Mike would take off and run through the grove of trees down an alleyway in the back of Aunt Teenie and Uncle Earl's house until he reached our backyard. By the time Mom reached the basketball court, all the guys would say, "Michael went home, Miss Idabel."

Mike would greet Mom as she came into the house, "Oh, hi Mama, I've been here." Michael was always in trouble for playing basketball when he should have been home. Even when he didn't get alerted that Mom was coming to get him, we all thought he would be embarrassed. He was not. Mike would just laugh and take whatever punishment got doled out and do it all over again.

Mom was the disciplinarian during the day, but if any of our misdeeds were deemed egregious, she would say, "Wait until your Daddy gets home." We knew we were in trouble for sure.

The playground had long ceased to be the center of George Mason's world. He worked and spent his money on clothes, books, and going to the beach with his Hall's Hill friends.

Summer's end was in sight. Year after year, we would remember how it felt. As kids, we reveled in every waking moment. We didn't know why we felt different; we just did. We were like flowers that bloomed, wild and free, soaking in the energy of the sun, growing a little taller, our skin a little browner from hours on the playground. Then we felt it all coming to an end—life was more restrained, less free, and more constricted. Just the same, it had been the best time of our lives.

CHAPTER 9

The Country Club

No one in my house was afraid of work. While Roz, Lynwood, Audrey, and I enjoyed the summer of 1958, George Mason and Mike had jobs. Mike worked odd jobs, cutting grass for neighbors and family. But George Mason worked outside of our community at a whites-only private establishment.

The Washington Golf and Country Club was a segregated club where wealthy white people golfed, swam, and attended social gatherings. It was only ten to fifteen minutes from our house. If you were Black, you were only allowed in as a worker, no matter your income. I've never been inside the country club, but I've driven by hundreds of times.

The private club sits on Glebe Road, one of Arlington's main thoroughfares, in an upscale neighborhood. It still retains its grandeur, replete with manicured grounds, large columns framing the circular driveway, valet donning a tuxedo-like uniform, waiting to greet the next guest or member arriving to mingle with the area's rich and famous.

Black folks did the cleaning, cooking, waiting, and bussing of tables. Others, like my dad and George Mason, worked as caddies and pool boys. And a few were valets, parking cars for big affairs. My dad first worked there as a teenager. That's also when George Mason began picking up weekend and summer work at the private club. On summer breaks from college, George sometimes returned to the club to earn money for school. Years later, as an adult, Dad caddied to make some extra money too.

Despite the extra income, neither Dad nor any Black men from our neighborhood worked at the club without knowing its history.

Shortly after the Civil War, a Black man named Moses Pelham Sr. purchased a large tract of land next to where the country club would later be built. He separated his land into plots and sold them to family members. That area would become known as Pelham Town. In 1888, Pressley Marion Rixey, US surgeon general for the Navy (1902-1910), bought the land adjoining Pelham Town for a summer home. Rixey later sold some acreage to the country club in 1907 and another portion to what is now Marymount University in 1924.[13]

Moses' grandson, William Pelham, was born in Pelham Town, and he owned property there until 1947. Everyone on Hall's Hill knew William. He attended Mount Salvation, and he was a deacon, which meant he had a position of power and respect within our community. In the 1920s, he left Pelham Town for Hall's Hill. William shared the story about the sale of his property in a *Washington Post* article about Hall's Hill: "Right after [World War II, the county] put in city water and said you had to be connected to it or you couldn't get an occupancy permit. But they wouldn't let me connect

13 "History," Washington Golf and Country Club, accessed September 19, 2020.

my house. The white people moving in didn't like my black tenants. So, I sold."[14]

Dad and the other adults on Hall's Hill understood the dichotomy they faced day to day, especially at the country club. The same white folks who went to great lengths to abscond Black folks' property, once "they" deemed it had value, might be the same people they worked for to earn extra money. Our community knew we had to walk a tight rope, but they didn't have to capitulate.

Instead, they funneled their displeasure into action, working to balance the scales of justice and equality, organizing and strategizing with the John M. Langston Citizens Association. Their goals were clear. They wanted access to the same educational resources, county services, and employment opportunities as Arlington's white residents. Black people knew the value of compartmentalizing their lives. There was no way to work at the Washington Golf and Country Club without understanding that reality.

You had to have a certain kind of demeanor to rise above the intentional rules designed to diminish your value. Dad and George Mason knew the country club rules had nothing to do with who they were, their intelligence, and their abilities. Their easy-going personalities proved to be a powerful source of strength while working in subservient roles among the privileged class.

"I started working at the country club when I was fourteen, and I worked there until I went to college. I had to get a work permit," George Mason recalled.

---

14 Hank Burchard, "Hall's Hill: Blacks Hold the High Ground," *The Washington Post*, February 27, 1969.

I asked George what it felt like to work at a place where his race prevented him from using the facilities. His response was funny yet brutally honest.

"It didn't matter that it was segregated. They just looked at you as a good *darkie*."

Dad and George Mason forged ahead, and over time, they connected with members who recognized their innate abilities. George Mason talked about how some members seemed to value Dad's abilities.

"Dad caddied. He worked on Saturdays and sometimes on Sundays. But Dad had regular golfers who would request that he caddy for them."

Dad was a very good golfer. He learned to play at Langston Golf Course, a Black public course in Washington, DC.

A young George Jones, Sr. (Dad) playing golf at Langston Golf Course in Washington, DC.

George Mason did a little bit of everything at the club. As a teen, he knew all of the Black people who worked there and what they did. It wasn't long before he would know many of the white people, especially those in positions of power.

"I started by just cleaning up—setting up tables for banquet and stuff like that. Then I started shining shoes." He helped a man named Clarence, who worked in the locker room at the club. Some of those experiences remain vivid memories. "Clarence Jones took care of the men's locker room, and his main job was to shine shoes. When the golfers came in, they left their shoes in front of their lockers. Clarence would go around and mark which locker the shoes came from. He cleaned and shined their shoes, and then put them back in front of the locker. I often worked with him."

George Mason set up for special events and waited tables. He worked from sunup to sundown, cleaning up from a previous night's event, setting up for that day's lunch or dinner. Then he would change into black slacks and a white shirt prescribed for wait staff so he could bus tables and wait on guests.

In later years, he would be assigned as a waiter at the swimming pool. That experience gave him entrance to another world.

"There were several families there that weren't that racist. I became friendly with Peter Olmstead's son. He owned Olmstead Oldsmobile on Wilson Boulevard. And Dr. Dolan's son. He's a doctor himself now. We all became friends. After I got off work, we would get together, and they would take me to parties with them in Georgetown."

George Mason was enterprising, and some of those relationships evolved into a small car wash business.

"Trust me, when I was working at the pool, their wives liked me. They would say George can you do so and so. And I washed their cars. I had about five customers whose cars I washed regularly. When their husbands came in from playing golf, they went to the Men's Grill to play cards. I'd bring their cars to our house, wash them, clean them up, and take them back."

For Dad, caddying at the country club was a side job. On the weekends during the summer, it would not be unusual to have someone call from the club to speak with Dad. If he wasn't there, we would let him know one of the country club members wanted him to caddy for them.

I never got the sense that either Dad or George Mason had any desire to play at the Washington Golf and Country Club, but caddies were later allowed to play there. While I don't know the exact date, the Washington Golf and Country Club eventually opened its membership to African Americans and other minorities.

Dad and his friends had their places to play golf. In addition to Langston Golf Course, by 1941, the interior secretary had desegregated all of DC's public golf courses. One of the city's nicest was the East Potomac Golf Course near the Tidal Basin.[15]

Dad played at East Potomac Golf course quite a bit. On weekends, he frequently went to the driving range there in the early evening. The course is near the Potomac River on Hains Point Island. To get there from Arlington, Dad drove

15 U.S. Department of Interior, National Park Service, *Links to the Past: A Historic Resource Study of National Park Service Golf Courses in the District of Columbia*, by Patricia Kuhn Babin, (November 2017).

past blocks of cherry blossom trees, and some of the city's historic and most visited sites, like the Jefferson Memorial and the Tidal Basin.

When Dad went to the driving range, I sometimes went along. I learned to play golf in high school. I knew how to hold a club, how to hit the ball, where to place my feet, and how to swing. I was always pretty strong, so I could hit the ball a good distance for a non-player. No one else had any interest in golf except George Mason, and he had moved away from home by the time Dad and I practiced at East Potomac.

Many African American men who lived on Hall's Hill played golf. In later years, the men's organization at Calloway Methodist Church created an annual golf tournament fundraiser. It was one of their most successful fundraising events. My husband played with them a few times, and he talked about how he had never seen anything like the tournament. "I've never seen so many Black golfers. It was amazing and inspiring."

Around one hundred Black golfers played in the tournament every year, including George Mason and almost all of Dad's golfing buddies from Hall's Hill.

For my dad and many of the men from Hall's Hill, the sport of golf as played at the Washington Golf and Country Club was a means to an end. George Mason and Mike worked at the club growing up, but Dad didn't see that kind of work as part of their future. He and men like him made sacrifices to create a better life for their children that didn't necessitate jobs at the country club and places like it. For Dad, getting a good education was the key to a better life for future generations.

CHAPTER 10

Becoming the Stratford Four

The Evening Star, Tuesday, September 2, 1958, headline read: *Arlington's School Case Heard, 30 Negroes Seek to Enter Seven White Institutions.* "Federal Judge Albert V. Bryan today convened court to determine whether thirty Negro students must be admitted to white Arlington schools for the fall term beginning Thursday."[16]

Despite the 1954 Supreme Court *Brown v. the Board of Education* ruling declaring "separate but equal has no place in public education," and its subsequent ruling in May 1955 that all schools should be integrated "with all deliberate speed," Virginia continued to resist efforts to integrate by developing workarounds to avoid the high court's rulings.

A lawsuit the NAACP had filed May 17, 1956 demanded that Arlington County schools integrate. The county appealed the suit several times, losing each appeal. Then September 14, 1957, the court decided to hear the case filed

16 Mary Lou Werner, "Arlington's School Case Heard, 30 Negroes Seek to Enter Seven White Institutions," *The Evening Star*, September 2, 1958.

on behalf of Arlington students by the NAACP. In support of the students, the NAACP requested a supplemental decree to direct Arlington County to admit the students named in the lawsuit.

The lead plaintiff in the case, Clarissa Thompson, and four of the seven co-plaintiffs, Stephen Thompson, E. Leslie Hamm, Louis Costley, Melvin Costley, and George Nelson, were all from Hall's Hill. The court granted the motion but withheld the order temporarily to allow the state of Virginia to appeal.[17]

Mom and several other parents received a summons from the court a couple of days after the court granted the motion. The subpoena ordered them to appear before the Committee on Law Reform and Racial activities in three days. They were required to testify about anti-NAACP laws passed during the Virginia lawmakers' session. The Hall's Hill community viewed the action as a ploy by the state to intimidate parents seeking to have their children admitted to Arlington's white schools. My sister writes in her book, *My Halls Hill Family: More Than a Neighborhood*, that my mother was "followed by the news media and made to feel extremely uncomfortable."[18]

At the time, I was only seven years old, but I remember seeing Mom and a couple of other parents on the evening news. The film revealed them bending down, attempting to avoid news cameras as they left the courtroom. Our mother was two months pregnant with her seventh child at the time. Little changed in our day-to-day life while the

17 Wilma Jones, *My Halls Hill Family: More Than a Neighborhood,* (New Providence, New Jersey: Bowker, October 10, 2018) p. 95-96.

18 Wilma Jones, *My Halls Hill Family: More Than a Neighborhood,* (New Providence, New Jersey: Bowker, October 10, 2018) p. 95-96.

controversy swirled, fueled by threats from racist groups throughout Arlington. They hoped their rhetoric would convince white parents to keep their kids from attending an integrated school.

On Wednesday, September 17, 1958, Judge Albert V. Bryan ruled in favor of four of the thirty applications for enrollment in a white Arlington school. While the ruling was favorable, he still gave the county until January to implement the action required. Based on the judge's decision, our brother, Michael, along with Ronald Deskins, Lance Newman, and Gloria Thompson, would attend H-B in September and transfer to Stratford Junior High on February 2, at the start of the second semester.[19]

It was the beginning of real change for Black residents in Hall's Hill, Green Valley, and Johnson's Hill. All three Black communities had been appealing to Arlington County for improved educational resources and facilities for Black public schools as far back as 1931. Their initial efforts had resulted in the establishment of Hoffman-Boston.[20]

If Mom and Dad had concerns about Mike's selection as one of the students to integrate Stratford, we never saw it. In the Jones house, life went on as it did before Judge Bryan's ruling.

For the first time in September 1958, all the Jones kids would be in school. Mike entered the seventh grade joining George Mason at H-B, who was now in the eleventh grade. There were still many Joneses at Langston. Roz began fifth

19 Mary Lou Werner, "Must Enroll Students in January '59: Board's Rejection of 26 Others Upheld by Bryan," *The Evening Star*, September 17, 1959.

20 Lindsey Bestebreurtje, "Built by People Themselves—African American Community Development in Arlington, Virginia, From Civil War through Civil Rights," (PhD diss., George Mason University, 2017), p.338.

grade, and Lynwood and I entered the second grade. Audrey started a two-year stint at Mother Goose Nursery School. She started there when she was four, turning five on October 17, 1958, which meant the next school year she would not meet Virginia's age cutoff; you had to be six by September 1.

Mike had been looking forward to moving on to H-B. While H-B was on Johnson's Hill, kids from Arlington's Black communities attended school there. Of the three neighborhoods, Green Valley had a larger Black community than Hall's Hill or Johnson's Hill. He wanted to play sports at H-B and get to know African American teenagers from Arlington's south side. Now, he would only spend four months there before transferring to Stratford.

Mike doesn't recall being conflicted about leaving H-B for Stratford, but Roz said he was. "Mike had a lot of fun that first semester at H-B. I think that was really difficult, not just for him, but for all four of them. The atmosphere at H-B was a lot of fun, and leaving that was hard."

Roz recalled a lot of discussion among the teachers at Langston, leading up to integration. "I remember the teachers at Langston showed us our test scores. I'm not sure if it was our standardized test, but it was something they would not have normally shared with us. They wanted us to know that when we went there that we had high test scores and that we were as smart as the white kids at Stratford."

But at that moment, nothing mattered except school, homework, and getting good grades. Life was normal again for everyone, including Mom, who returned to work at the Langston cafeteria—pregnant and all.

The school year lacked the freedom of summer, but it was not devoid of amusement. Between Halloween, likely school closings for snowstorms, and a long Christmas break, we recaptured some of the carefree days we had left behind.

Halloween was mostly about making the best homemade costume and trick or treating with your friends. It was a rare school night when we were out after dark, literally running the streets with neighborhood friends. For Mike and his buddies, Halloween was a chance to have fun mocking the invisible barriers imposed by segregation.

"When we got older, we would put on our Halloween mask and go into the white section to trick or treat. They didn't know who you were. It was great fun. We got all the candy we wanted, and it would last you for weeks," Mike recalls.

Nothing beat Christmas, but the anticipation of a big snowstorm was a close second, mostly since schools often closed for as long as a week. The county cleaned the main thoroughfares first, then the neighborhoods. The Black communities were always the last to be plowed.

We had four streets with at least one hill, and some had two. There was an unspoken order about where kids went to sleigh ride and the time of day it was acceptable to be there. In the daytime, elementary school kids rode the hills, mostly on Dinwiddie Street. And the bravest (and reckless) kids came out at night to sled down Cameron Street.

We couldn't wait to get out on the hills. We put on layer after layer of socks, and sweaters, then gloves and a hat. We must have looked like the Michelin Man walking up the street. After hours of gliding down, falling in the snow, every layer of clothing wet, and our hands, feet, and faces cold, we went home. Into the small bathroom, shivering and wet, we took off the wet clothes. We hung them on the shower curtain rod, got something to eat, changed our clothes, and went back out to do it all over again.

On Dinwiddie Street, you could slow down halfway, but on Cameron Street, you had to sleigh ride from the top all the way down until you got to the red apartments. The teenagers owned Cameron Street at night. It didn't matter how cold it was, they gathered around a fire made in a big oil can to warm their hands, and with every breath, the steel cold air streamed from their mouths.

Once they warmed up, they picked up the sled, some grabbed the bumper of a passing car to accelerate their sledding, took off down the hill, let go, and flew on down the next incline. The first snow day that you thought you were brave enough to hang out with the "big kids," you would head up to Cameron Street at night and give it a try. I don't think I ventured up there more than once or twice, but my brothers were there often.

Our Christmas school break lasted for several weeks. But we never got our tree until Christmas Eve. It was a tradition I thought that was true for all families. As we waited for Dad to get home from work, we would pop popcorn and sit in front of the fireplace with a needle and thread stringing it together. We used our string of popcorn, tinsel, lights, and ornaments to decorate our tree.

When Dad arrived home, he usually had a big, beautiful, and perfectly shaped tree, but sometimes it would be a bit wonky. Roz said, Dad would wait until the Christmas tree lots closed to get a free tree. Most lots closed around six in the evening because the owners wanted to get home to be with their family. When the lots closed, trees always remained. Dad saved money wherever he could.

Once the tree was up, we could barely contain our excitement. There wouldn't be a present anywhere in sight, but we believed that Santa was coming. Before we went to bed, we put cookies and milk out and reminded Mom and Dad to put the fire out so Santa could come down the chimney.

Early in the morning, around two or three, Roz, Mike, Lynwood, and I would sneak down to the living room to get presents. If Mom happened to hear us, she would usually let us open one gift before sending us back to bed. We went back to sleep until later in the morning when we awoke and spent the remainder of the day opening the rest of our gifts.

On Christmas morning, there were always more gifts under the tree than imaginable. It was everything we could have hope for and truly unforgettable. It seemed like in every corner of the room packages were stacked on top of the other. We giggled. Looking back and forth at each other, all we could do was smile. Then the treasure hunt began as we looked through all the boxes to find the packages with our names on them. Not every box under the tree was for us. There were gifts for uncles and aunts, and for Dad and Mom's godchild, Warren. He was the son of Lynwood and my godmother, Mrs. Adele.

Sometimes there were so many boxes we had to step between and over them. Stockings filled with fruit and nuts were on the mantle, along with new dresses and coats on hangers. We always got lots of toys and clothes. I'm not sure how Mom and Dad bought all seven of us everything we wanted, plus new clothes, but they did. Every year until we stopped believing in Santa, we had a wonderful, almost-storybook Christmas morning.

First Steps Toward Equality

Following the Christmas of 1958, we returned to school. The start of that semester was never more important for any student or community than it was for Mike, Gloria, Lance, and Ronnie and Hall's Hill. At twelve years old, the four were at the center of an equal rights storm. Their success would open the door for every Black child in Arlington County. A lot was riding on their ability to show the world just how intelligent and capable they were.

On the morning of February 2, 1959, they gathered at Ronnie's house, whose dad drove them to Stratford Junior High school. I'm sure our parents were nervous, and the whole neighborhood was on alert. The neo-Nazi party based in Arlington had continued to make inflammatory remarks opposing the integration of Stratford. Community members and other advocates for integration feared they might cause trouble.

Up to this point, no African American had received approval to attend or be admitted to a white school in Arlington. Driving up to Stratford, a fifteen to twenty-minute ride from Hall's Hill, Mike and the other students saw police on every corner while approaching the school. Members of the Arlington Police Department bomb squad were on hand as well as many patrolmen. The four teens entered the school together, went to the office to check in, and had an escort take them to their classrooms.

While the resources Black schools received were not equal to white schools, academically, the four students were on par with their white counterparts. Mike credited the excellent teachers and instruction they received at Langston for much of their academic success at Stratford. "When I got to class, I found their work wasn't much harder than what I was doing before. The teachers we had at Langston were great. They had high standards, and their teaching excellence is what laid the foundation for our success at Stratford. That's why we were chosen as the four students to attend Stratford, because of the great teachers at Langston."

During their four months at H-B, Mike and the other students indulged in collegiate sports, school dances, and a social life synonymous with junior high school and adolescence. Attending Stratford would deprive them of the very things that made being a teenager so special. The Arlington County School board did not want Black students socializing or competing in athletics with the white students. In the first few years of integration, the school board banned all intramural sports and social activities.

So much about growing up on Hall's Hill prepared Mike to deal with the covert racism he experienced at Stratford. "It didn't matter what happened at Stratford because I always knew I could go home. It was like going to school with people you didn't know at first. But it was just school."

Mike and most of the kids on Hall's Hill had an inner fortitude ingrained in them. "No matter what was going on at Stratford, which didn't amount to much, I came back to Hall's Hill, where I had a nice group of friends and a loving community. Because of Hall's Hill and the people around me, I was able to do well at Stratford."

Each year, a few more Black students entered Arlington's previously all-white schools. In the future, the four teenagers from Hall's Hill would become known as The Stratford Four.

The new baby arrived one month after Mike entered Stratford. Mom and Dad's seventh and last child was born on March 7, 1959. They named her Wilma. When Mike was born, George Mason wasn't pleased, and much like him, Audrey wasn't happy about no longer being the baby of the family. To make it even worse, she thought Mom brought the wrong baby home. Upon seeing her very fair and bald-headed sister, Audrey asked Mom, "Why did you bring this white baby home?" We all laughed.

It was an adjustment having an infant in the house. As we looked around the neighborhood, it seemed like a few other women had the same idea. Several of Mom's friends, including Aunt Pat, also welcomed babies in 1959. It had been a busy and eventful year in the Jones household. Before we knew it, it would be summer all over again.

CHAPTER 11

Church Life

Throughout our youth, we spent many hours at Mount Salvation Baptist Church. Our church life was an integral part of our being. It was interconnected with our family life, weaved together like a quilt, taking form over the course of our lives, shaping our thoughts, actions, and viewpoints into one complete image of the people we would become.

When Roz thought back to growing up, she said, "Mount Salvation was kind of our life." Our connection to the church was so pervasive that teenagers on Hall's Hill would often say, "If the doors of the church are open, there's a Jones there."

As the oldest girl in the family, Mom expected a lot of Roz. She had a connection to nearly every youth activity. If the organization had junior in front of the name, Roz was probably a member. She was a junior usher, a junior missionary, in the junior choir, and she attended Baptist Training Union. Roz also went with Mom to Wednesday night prayer meeting and Sunday school teacher's meetings. Eventually, she played piano for the Youth Chorus Choir, the Senior Choir, and Sunday School.

Looking back, it seemed like she was a miniature of Mom. It wasn't as if Mike and George Mason weren't active in the church; they were. Lynwood, Audrey, and I, later joined many of the same organizations, and Wilma followed in our footsteps. But no one matched Roz's level of involvement.

Most of us took piano lessons when we were growing up, Roz, Audrey, Lynwood, and me. But none of us transitioned into a real pianist, except Roz. Most of us stuck with our lessons for a couple of years and then stopped playing. But Roz continued. In my mind, that was intentional on Roz's part, but I would later realize that was far from true. She later shared her motivation with me. "I never wanted to continue playing the piano. I liked it, but not enough to continue on."

Uncle Dede wanted Roz to play for the Sunday School. Playing an instrument and becoming more proficient required practice, so he decided to surprise Roz with a brand-new mahogany piano. "When Dede bought me that piano, I felt I had no choice. What else could I do, but continue to play," Roz said.

The delivery men placed the beautiful mahogany furniture in our modest-sized living room. It was brand new, and it looked expensive. The sofa and chairs in the living room were simple and understated, which drew your eyes toward the lovely musical instrument as soon as you entered our house. I remember thinking, "Why does Roz get a piano?" It wasn't about the piano. It was such an expensive gift. Until I began writing this book, I had no idea that the piano was one gift Roz would have preferred not to receive.

Our connection with the church gave us exposure to places outside of our neighborhood. Mrs. Hazel's husband and Jimmy's dad, Reverend Browne, was very invested in creating venues for Black youth to expand their purview. He was committed to exposing young people to new places, new people, and new experiences. Through his relationship with the Northern Virginia Baptist Association, an organization of Black churches, established in 1878, Reverend Browne was one of the members who advocated for creating a sleepaway camp. It would offer Black youth a place to experience the world beyond our neighborhoods and help them develop a sense of independence and confidence. He successfully achieved his goal with the creation of the Baptist Center camp.

Every summer, at least one of us went to the Baptist Center. Roz was the first to go, then Lynwood and I went, followed by Audrey and later Wilma. Most of us liked camp while others like me and Mike, who had visited an earlier sleepaway camp, didn't find it to our liking.

The Baptist Center was in a remote location, miles away from commercial businesses and residential communities, and hours away from our home. Kids came from all over Northern Virginia to spend a week or two. My first and only experience at camp was not one I wanted to relive. Lynwood and I were there together, but he had friends like Jimmy there to hang out with. I don't recall knowing any of the girls. Mom and Dad had paid for Lynwood and me to attend camp for two weeks. Fortunately for me, I had to go home for a piano recital at the end of the first week. I begged Mom and Dad not to make me go back.

Roz and Lynwood both enjoyed camp and went on to be counselors, as did Audrey and Wilma. More than any of us, Audrey and Wilma were die-hards. As kids, they were at the Baptist Center every chance they got.

Audrey had to convince Mom to let her go away to camp. Because of my negative experience, Mom wasn't sure Audrey would like it there. But Audrey refused to take no for an answer. She worried Mom about going until she finally gave in. Once Audrey went to the Baptist Center, it became a summer destination she anxiously looked forward to from the time she was nine until the age of fifteen. She started as a camper and then became a counselor.

For Audrey, the camp gave her a sense of freedom and independence she had not enjoyed anywhere else. Hanging out with her friends Shermane and Gail, sleeping and cooking outside was Audrey's idea of fun. There was no one to tell the campers what clothes to wear or how to comb their hair. Outside of following the camp's rules, all the decisions were up to each camper. She made new friends and had a chance to learn leadership skills watching and listening to the teens who were counselors like she would one day become.

Wilma benefited from many of the same experiences as Audrey. She first visited the camp when Mom and Dad took Audrey for one of her two-week stays there. "When I was about five years old, I rode with Mom and Dad to drop Audrey off at camp, and I hid under a bed in the older girls' barracks. In my mind, I thought they would leave me, and I would get to stay at camp. Of course, they found me, and I went home with them," Wilma said.

Like Audrey, Wilma had friends that went to the camp at the Baptist Center. Wilma's best friend, Cheryl, was the grandchild of Reverend Browne, and he was the camp director. Even before Wilma became a camper, she spent time at the Baptist Center. Reverend Browne often took Cheryl with him to the camp, and Wilma went along to keep her company. You had to be eight years old to attend camp, and both Wilma and Cheryl were there every year that they were eligible. Wilma learned to swim at camp and later became the lifeguard there.

The Baptist Center gave Wilma a chance to gain leadership skills and develop confidence. But she remembers it being in a much more structured way than Audrey had experienced: "When I was thirteen, Reverend Browne got me on the Northern Virginia Baptist Association board as a Youth representative. I'm not sure how he did it, but it gave me a chance to have a big speaking role there. All of the association's events were at the Baptist Center, so I spent time there beyond summer camp."

The Baptist Center wasn't a fancy camp. It wasn't the trappings or decor that drew kids back year after year. It was what they learned about life, themselves, and others. It was a space where Black youth like Wilma and Audrey learned how to be resilient, confident youth and gained skills they would build upon for the rest of their lives. For two weeks every summer, they escaped the cocoon of their parents' watchful eyes to make mistakes, learn from them, and grow up a little more each year.

At the end of the summer of 1960, our family dynamics began to change. Soon George Mason would leave us to go off to college. It would feel different not having him around. Because George Mason was so much older than most of us, our lives had not intersected in the same way, but we saw our future through him in many ways. If George Mason did something, we looked forward to growing up and emulating him. Simultaneous with his departure, Roz was entering Stratford Junior High with Michael. For Roz, starting junior high school at Stratford was as exciting as George Mason going to college.

"Before I went to Stratford, I had this idea of having a different experience than the one Mike described where you went to school and just did your schoolwork and then came back to your neighborhood. In my mind, I had these visions that you would go there and meet people, and they would become your friends. That's not what happened. People weren't really mean, but they were not trying to be your friend."

Our family and community's involvement in the move towards integration heightened our awareness of national and world events. The 1960s presidential campaign of John F. Kennedy and Richard Nixon was a news story that interested our parents and us. As Walter Cronkite reported nightly on the upcoming election, John Kennedy's youthfulness and liberal perspectives attracted our attention and kept us interested in the campaign. During this time, I heard my Dad say he was going to vote for Richard Nixon. I couldn't understand why.

"Daddy, why would you vote for Richard Nixon? I think you should vote for Kennedy. He's a Democrat," I said.

"Yes, Kennedy is a Democrat but has vowed to cut budgets that would force the closing of the factory at the Washington Navy Yard if elected. I'm voting for Nixon. We have a better chance of the Navy Yard's Weapons Plant staying open."

This discussion with my dad was probably the first political conversation I ever had with my parents. On Tuesday, November 8, 1960, John F. Kennedy became the thirty-fifth president of the United States. For the rest of the year, I imagine Dad must have been on pins and needles. He must have wondered if the president-elect would follow through on his campaign promise to cut budgets impacting his place of employment.

Whatever worry or concern our parents had was totally opaque to us. They shielded us from adult concerns and issues. In our house, we were allowed to be kids. They surrounded us with a positive environment and a belief in what was good and right. Ultimately, they handled concerns about the future with a commitment to their faith.

At church, we also participated in secular type activities centered around a religious message. We learned about acting, theater, music, and production through our Christmas play and recitations. Mom always played a significant role in bringing these productions to life with our neighbor, Mrs. Hamm.

Her family lived directly in back of ours and her husband was an architect who worked for the federal government. Their house was more contemporary and newer than ours, incorporating Frank Lloyd Wright's architectural design aesthetic. They had three kids: one a little younger than George Mason, another around Roz's age, and their youngest the same age as Wilma.

For the most part, Black people could not purchase homes in more upscale neighborhoods because of segregation. So, it was common for Black people from all economic strata to live in the same community. There were doctors, architects, college professors, and other professionals living and socializing with the mailman, journeyman, carpenters, barbers, and hairdressers. We all lived and worked together and respected each other's skills and abilities. But most of all, our families were friends.

Mrs. Hamm and Mom talked on the telephone, met at the church, or in each other's homes for weeks to pull everything together for the big production. It was like a mini community theater. It didn't have professional lighting, but people were assigned to turn the lights up and down to create drama and emotion at the appropriate time. Mom made sure any kids who wanted to be a part of the program had a role.

They reached out to all the talented people in the community to help create a dramatic and impactful production. Mom might contact Uncle Clarence to lend his carpentry skills.

"Clarence, can you build a manger for the Christmas play?"

"Sure, Idabel. When do you need it?"

"At least a week before the program. Let me know what you need from me."

They would think about who they knew who could draw and paint and ask them to create the backdrop depicting Bethlehem.

Anyone who had sewing skills made robes and costumes, including Roz and me, when I was older. It was an honor to be able to do more than be in the program.

For weeks every Saturday, Mom and Mrs. Hamm would rehearse the play. It was each parent's responsibility to make sure their children memorized their recitations. They would rehearse the entire production, music, recitations, curtains, and lighting a couple of weeks before the day of the event.

On the night of the program, the church was always full. And, when it was over, all the youth involved felt a sense of accomplishment.

The Christmas program helped us recognize how our faith didn't mean we had to eliminate arts, culture, and social engagement from our lives. We didn't need to separate ourselves from the church to enjoy some of the same recreational activities as others. As we remained close to our church family and activities, it built character and resolve about the importance of a spiritual relationship.

Our parents knew that one day we would face conflicts and tests. If they could help us appreciate all the ways the church had enriched our lives through our association with the choir, as ushers, in Sunday School, at camp, and annual Christmas and Easter programs, we might begin to understand the value of faith and have access to a power greater than ourselves.

CHAPTER 12

The First Jones Attends College

Throughout high school, George Mason's personality and athletic prowess had served him well. He had been a popular, well-liked, good student and athlete. George Mason, who was now about five feet, eleven inches, still looked a lot like Dad. He was slim, with an athletic build, dark skin, and of course, the telling Jones nose. Both Mom and Dad had distinctive noses, although Mom's was a bit sharper and more pointed.

Somehow, George Mason had kept everything in balance, maintaining a good grade point average while managing school and sports demands. Watching George Mason's progression and now his big move toward college impressed his young sister, Roz. "I always thought George Mason was super cool. He was my big brother, and everybody liked him. When he started talking about going to college, it became something I wanted to do too."

Before George Mason headed off to Stillman College in Tuscaloosa, Alabama, he also had a scholarship offer to attend Norfolk State College in Norfolk, Virginia. But his choices disappeared when he allowed social and sports activities to cloud his priorities in the spring semester. He missed Norfolk State's deadline for accepting their scholarship offer. The choice was made for him by default. No one in our family had ever heard of Stillman, and no one had visited Alabama. Suddenly, things had gone from being exciting to a little scary.

In 1960, the year he graduated from high school, civil rights demonstrations were taking place all over the south. In February of 1960, four African American students in Greensboro, North Carolina, had staged a nonviolent protest at a segregated Woolworth's lunch counter. Those protests continued through July of 1960. It was unfamiliar territory for our family. George Mason going off to college was important, but so was his safety. We were concerned about how far Alabama was from home and that it was not the most welcoming place for a Black male teenager.

George Mason's Hoffman Boston High School graduation picture

Dad, Mom, and George Mason all felt confident things would work out, and they prepared to get him ready for a successful trip and first year at college. Close family friends like George Mason's godfather, James Scott, whom everyone just referred to as "Scott," helped ensure he was ready for the nearly 800-mile trip to college.

George Mason spent a lot of time at Scott's house. He lived close to Grandma Jones' in a small but contemporary brick house. Scott had a beautiful white Austen Healy sports car that George Mason often had a chance to drive.

As he prepared to leave for college, George Mason packed all of his clothes in a steamer trunk given to him by Scott. It was like a traveling wardrobe, with drawers, hanging racks, and compartments to store your clothes. The twenty-hour train trip to Tuscaloosa would mark the first time he had traveled anywhere by train. His arrival in Alabama introduced him to a level of animus he would not soon forget. "When we arrived in Alabama, I was the only person getting off in Tuscaloosa. I got off the train, and I waited for the porters to hand my trunk down to me. Instead, the porter just kicked the trunk over the side of the train," George said.

He thought to himself, "Welcome to Tuscaloosa."

He took a taxi to campus and knocked on the coach's door, who directed him to his room. In less than a month, George Mason was back at the coach's door. But this time, he was there to express his misgivings about attending Stillman.

As the coach greeted George Mason, he informed him he wanted to go home and asked if he could use his telephone to call Dad. George Mason's conversation with Dad went something like this.

"Hi Dad, this is George Mason."

Dad said, "What's wrong?"

George Mason told Dad, "I don't like it, and I'm not happy."

As he spoke to Dad, the coach yelled out in the background, "Tell your father he will owe us $895!"

Dad heard the coach say something and asked, "What did he say?"

George Mason told him what the coach said, and Dad replied, "No, tell him we won't owe him anything!" Then he hung up the phone.

George Mason recalled, "I adjusted, and the rest was history!"

He was attending Stillman on a baseball scholarship. Mom and Dad were raising seven kids, George Mason, the oldest, and the youngest only one year old. They didn't have a thousand dollars to repay Stillman College for defaulting on a scholarship because George Mason didn't like it there. He was going to have to find a way to make it work. In George Mason's own words, "it was different, really different."

Stillman's campus was more rural than Arlington. There were large areas of land and open spaces with cows and a few buildings. Arlington was more suburban. There were no farms, and the days when people had chickens and horses had long passed. Even the way students dressed was different. Many male students wore overalls—a very different look than the hip attire George Mason and his classmates from H-B wore or aspired to wear. The alpaca sweaters or button-down collar shirts and shiny slim leg slacks the cool boys wore in Washington, DC, and nearby Arlington, were nowhere to be found.

Once George Mason started playing baseball, he came to love college. He especially loved pitching for the team, but those days were short-lived after injuring his arm in his sophomore year. He wasn't out on the field any longer, but the coach had other plans for him. He recognized what a hard worker George Mason was and kept him involved by making him the head of the athletic work program. He made friends and had long since put those early days of giving up on Stillman and leaving Alabama behind him.

By 1961, George Mason and other Black students in Alabama joined the sit-ins and nonviolent protests that first started in Greensboro, North Carolina. "I never knew white folks that were so nasty! We would march and hold demonstrations to protest segregation that was still in place in Alabama. One of the things I learned was not to be on the edge of the marchers. I made sure I was near the middle. If you were on the edges, the white people would have bleached hair poles with nails on the end, and they would poke you with the nails, just enough to hurt but not penetrating your skin. Being in Alabama at that time was something," George recalled. Student demonstrations and sit-ins were just one of the fronts in the fight for equal rights in Alabama.

In 1963, three miles from Stillman College, the University of Alabama became the focus of national media attention. Then-Governor George Wallace stood in the university's doorway to prevent Vivian Malone and James Hood from integrating the college. Wallace's efforts were unsuccessful. Supported by federalized guardsmen, Malone and Hood entered the university four hours later.[21]

21 "Scholarship Recipients: Vivian Malone Jones," NAACP Legal Defense and Educational Fund, accessed September 29, 2020.

George Mason's freshman year roommate, Mack, had been hired to be a driver for Vivian. From that encounter, Mack and Vivian started dating and later got married. George's friendship with Mack and Vivian grew, and they also became friends of our family.

George Mason was always a good-hearted person. When classmates were coming toward the northeast and didn't have a place to stay, he would invite them to stay at our house. To this day, when we reminisce about how much fun it was to have his friends at our home, we still can't remember where we all slept. With nine family members, one bathroom, and whomever George Mason brought home from college, somehow, we made it work. His college friend from West Virginia, also named George, would spend the night after driving them home from Alabama. Other friends, like Herman, and Mack stayed for an extended period.

Herman was an international student from Panama. It was too far and too expensive for him to go home for the holidays. So, George Mason, being a good-hearted person, brought Herman home. George Mason thought back on those times. "He didn't have any place to go during the holiday; he was a nice dude. We didn't hang out a lot in college, but we were friends. So, when I found out he didn't have any place to go, I told him to come home with me." It was always exciting to have company, and Herman was not like anyone we had ever met, mostly because he was from another country, and he spoke Spanish fluently.

We enjoyed having Herman with us and learning a little about Panama, which was fortuitous. George Mason spent most of his Christmas break out with his friends from home and partying. Herman wasn't much of a party guy, so he spent hours in front of the television and at home with us. He especially loved a 1960s television classic *Amos 'n' Andy*. With only one TV in the house, it was a sacrifice for a house full of teenagers and elementary-age kids to give up our TV time, but we did it. Herman was our guest, and we wanted to make him feel at home. To this day, we all consider Herman's stay one of our fondest childhood memories.

When he graduated from Stillman in June 1965, my parents didn't attend George Mason's graduation, probably because they couldn't afford to. We were all proud of him, but we were excited to have him back at home more than anything. He had given us great memories and a glimpse of college life.

Once George Mason arrived back home, Mack, originally from Florida, came North in search of a job and stayed with our family. Mack was a very tall, thin guy with a mellow disposition and a fun spirit. He had a black convertible Chevrolet Impala that he often pulled around to our large backyard to wash and wax. He truly became part of our family, especially upon George Mason being notified of his draft into the Army on July 28, 1965.

The Vietnam War was going on and the government wasted no time drafting young Black men as soon as their deferments expired. After George Mason completed basic training, he received his orders: he would be going to Vietnam. When he relayed the news to Mom and told her he didn't think he would be coming back, Mom dismissed that thought. "Oh, boy, you'll be back!" Our parents always chose to have a positive point of view. As my sister recounts in her book, *My Halls Hill Family: More Than A Neighborhood*, "Moma would always tell us to look on the bright side."[22]

George Mason during his military service *(left)*. George Mason at home in his Army uniform *(right)*.

We were all sad and, of course, concerned about George Mason going to Vietnam. It just seemed so unfair. He had just arrived back home, and now he was gone again, but this time to a more dangerous place. In so many ways, our earlier concerns about civil rights demonstrations looked insignificant. Mack didn't get drafted, and he continued to live at our house until the fall. His girlfriend, Vivian Malone, also came North to work that summer, and George Mason arranged for her to stay at Scott's house. Mack and Vivian remained friends of our family until their passing.

George Mason had paved the way for the rest of us to see college as something possible for us too. Like Roz, we all wanted to be like George Mason. We all aspired to go to college.

22 Wilma Jones, *My Halls Hill Family: More Than a Neighborhood.* (New Providence: Bowker, October 10, 2018) p. 42.

CHAPTER 13

Losing the Ones We Love

In January 1961, John Fitzgerald Kennedy took office as the thirty-fifth president of the United States. In addition to the budget cuts Kennedy had campaigned on, the factory where Dad worked could not conform to new technological approaches in manufacturing munitions.

The Bureau of Ordnance was the organization responsible for oversight of the facility. They saw few options for keeping the facility open. Early in 1962, the government announced a reduction-in-force of employees, and the century-old Naval Gun Factory at the Washington Navy Yard began closing down.[23]

Dad had seven kids and a wife to care for. He didn't have the luxury of waiting to be laid off. Dad began looking for machinist positions close to home long before the

23 Washington Navy Yard, Human Resources Office, *History of the Washington Navy Yard Civilian Workforce 1799-1962*, by John G. Sharp, (Washington, D.C., 2003).

reduction-in-force started. With no success finding anything comparable to his current job, he expanded his search beyond the Washington metropolitan area.

Shortly after Kennedy assumed his role as president, Dad accepted a job at the New York Shipbuilding Company in Camden, New Jersey. Knowing Dad, I'm sure he had concerns about leaving Mom alone with the six of us. And Mom, well, I can hear her now: "George, go ahead and accept the job. We'll be just fine."

Dad commuted between Arlington, Virginia, and Camden, New Jersey, from early 1961 through mid-1962.

Things were very different without him at home every night. He took the job in New Jersey to ensure we would continue to have all of the material things we needed. But we still missed the casual conversations about school and hearing him remind Mike and Lynwood to take out the trash. We missed the ordinary things we never knew could be gone, if only temporarily. And worst of all, we had no idea when life would return to normal.

We had become accustomed to a certain rhythm on Sundays. We went to church, ate dinner together, and ended the day watching *The Ed Sullivan Show.* Instead of a lazy afternoon complaining about attending school in the morning, it became a time to say goodbye as Dad departed for New Jersey.

Fridays were just the opposite. There was a feeling of genuine glee. When we got home from school, we counted down to Dad's arrival. Lynwood and I had a tradition to build up to the moment when we would see Dad again.

After we got home from school on Fridays, we went to the record player and began playing a forty-five single by a Black doo-wop group, Shep and the Limelites. The group was enjoying a period of success with their Billboard charting single, "Daddy's Home." The song was a love letter of sorts from a guy to his girlfriend, but we ignored the lyrics referencing the guy's girlfriend and focused on the chorus that expressed how we felt about our *daddy* coming home.

As we waited for him to arrive, we would sing along with the record in anticipation. Dad coming home for the weekend was the most significant part of every week. Until he arrived, we imagined that moment of bliss by singing and playing that song over and over again. As it got closer to the time for him to get home, we would pull back the curtains, peep out the window periodically, waiting for Dad's car to pull into the driveway. When the car turned into the driveway, we were out of the door. He couldn't get out of the car fast enough for us.

"Hiiii Daddy," Lynwood and I yelled as we jumped on Dad's legs. He would walk toward the front door with both of us clinging to him.

As soon as Dad got home, we all wanted to show him how much we missed him and find out what we could do for him. One of my jobs was to help Dad remove the ingrown hairs on his face from shaving. When he was home for the weekend, he would ask me, "Hey Lydia, do you want to help me by pulling the ingrown hairs from my face?"

I didn't mind at all. "Sure, Dad!"

He would lay back on the bed, and I would get a pair of tweezers and a roll of toilet paper. I leaned across his chest and Dad would point out the places the hair was ingrown. I would pull them out one by one. It was my special job, and I loved doing it.

By 1962, Dad had been working in New Jersey for almost a year. We learned to accept the necessary sacrifice until he was able to get a job closer to home. It helped that family would sometimes stop by to visit.

Whenever we heard a knock at the door, you would think we had never seen people before. It's likely Mom was in the kitchen or the basement washing clothes. We were probably all in our little corners of the world reading a book or in the backyard. Whoever was in the house and heard the sound of *knock, knock, knock* raced to open the door, and one of us would yell, "Somebody's at the *door*!" And then, we would peep through one of the three small windowpanes in the door to see who was there.

It was usually a family member like Uncle Earl, our Dad's cousin; he lived three houses up Dinwiddie Street from us. Or it might be Mom's brother, Uncle Clarence, or her sister, Aunt Beanie, whose real name was Erroll.

Their occasional visits helped fill the space when Dad was working in New Jersey. It was always a treat when they visited. Each of them was different, and they enriched our lives. Uncle Earl would almost always come by early in the morning, and you never saw him without a cigar in his mouth. It probably wasn't lit, but it was almost always with him. He might have been in his fifties and not too tall, probably about five feet, eight inches. Uncle Earl usually wore a nice felt hat with a grosgrain ribbon above the brim.

He was an easygoing man and had a pleasant disposition. Mostly he would sit and chat with Mom when Dad wasn't there. We were allowed to sit for a bit and talk with him and Mom. Uncle Earl was a tailor by profession, but he also did many odd jobs, like working at Chinn's Funeral Parlor and making Adirondack chairs and benches. He would stay for an hour and then "head on back up the street."

When Uncle Clarence came by, if we happened to look out the living room window before opening the door, we knew it was him because we would see his pickup truck parked in front of the house. He typically wore overalls with pencils in the small pockets at the top portion of his overalls. Uncle Clarence probably wasn't overweight, but he no longer retained the slim physique of his youth. If Lynwood opened the door, he would greet him with a big smile, "Hi! Uncle Clarence!"

He would ask where Mom was, "Where's Idabel?"

Lynwood would say, "She's in the kitchen."

"Hey, Idabel, what do you need me to help you with?"

And, he proceeded to help Mom with tasks or repairs she wanted him to work on. But he never left without spending a few moments with us. Oftentimes, he would play a couple of songs he knew on an old white piano that sat in the bedroom that had been George Mason's. They were honky-tonk type songs, and he would bang away at that piano while we sat or stood around listening and laughing.

When Aunt Beanie came by, she would talk with Mom for a while, and then she would ask, "Idabel, can the kids go with me to the zoo?"

"Sure, Beanie, if they want to go," said Mom.

And, Aunt Beanie would say, "Woodie, Lydia, Audrey, and Wilma, you want to ride with me to the zoo?" We all called Lynwood, Woodie, sometimes.

Of course, we all said yes. Then Aunt Beanie would tell us, "Go get dressed, and let's go!"

We would jump in whatever cool car she was driving at the time. For a while, she had a convertible. She might put the top down, turn the music up, and off we would go.

An earlier trip to the National Zoo with Aunt Beanie. Audrey is in the front, Lynwood is behind her, and Lydia is holding Wilma.

Dad's sister, Almeda—Aunt Meme to us—really enjoyed sharing some of the fruits and vegetables she canned over the summer, and we sometimes visited her house.

Having our aunts and uncles stop by was helpful for Mom while Dad was working in New Jersey. By mid-1962, Dad had finally landed a job in Maryland at the US Naval Propellant Plant. One thing Dad and Mom realized when he returned home was that their money would only stretch so far. It became evident that even Dad's new job and Mom's part-time job wouldn't be enough for our present or future needs like college. The days of passing clothes down were pretty much over. Dad often found he needed to buy four or five new pairs of shoes and coats at once. It wasn't long before he took on a part-time job in the evenings working as a custodian at a couple of small banks in McLean, Virginia.

Shortly before Dad found work closer to home, Nana and Grandma Jones' health grew worse. Grandma Jones was now eighty-eight years old. Nana was seventy-eight.

Lynwood remembered how Mom helped Nana when she was ill. "When Nana got sick, Moma would go up and take care of her. They would sit in the kitchen, and Mom would wash her hair. Sometimes, she would help her attend to sores that she got on her back."

Nana's health grew more severe in April. She was diagnosed with pneumonia and admitted to Freedman's Hospital. Mom, Uncle Clarence, Uncle Dede, and Aunt Beanie visited her throughout the approximate one-week stay. They took us with them to see her too.

Audrey remembers the last time she saw Nana. She was with Uncle Clarence as they visited her in the large ward at Freedman's Hospital. "When we entered the ward, Uncle Clarence said, do you see her? I just saw a whole bunch of light-skinned women, and I pointed to the one I thought was her. He said, no, that's not her, and then pointed her out to me. That was the last time I saw her."

I'm not sure of the exact date, but Nana died in April 1962. Even as an eleven year old, I felt the void and sadness. For days after her funeral, I thought about her. One of the songs from the funeral, *In the Sweet By and By*, kept spinning through my head. I missed her terribly. What must it have felt like for Mom, Aunt Beanie, Uncle Clarence, and Uncle Dede, if it felt this bad for me?

As soon as Nana passed, Mom and her siblings were concerned about where Uncle Dede would live. Dede's Parkinson's disease condition meant he couldn't live alone. The disease affected his movements, most notably, his hands shook. He worked every day and was self-sufficient, except for things that required having a steady hand, like cooking. Not long after Nana's passing, Dede moved in with Aunt Beanie. It didn't work as well as he expected, and he asked Mom if he could move in with us. Dede became a part of our nuclear family. We were all excited to have him with us.

There were two bedrooms on the first floor of our house. Mom and Dad slept in one, and Dede moved into the other. George Mason was away at college, but there were still six kids in our house. Mike and Lynwood shared the first bedroom upstairs. Rosalind, Audrey, Wilma, and I shared the bigger bedroom in the back.

Uncle Dede had always been present in our lives. We saw him weekly when we went grocery shopping, at Nana's house, and in church every Sunday. But his involvement in our lives was even more profound, first with Roz and Mike and then later with Lynwood and me.

Uncle Dede saw that there were things we missed out on by living in Arlington because of segregation. He worked in DC and realized there were many cultural and entertainment opportunities we couldn't experience as kids and he went out of his way to expose Roz and Mike to movie theaters and simple pleasures they couldn't enjoy in Arlington.

Roz recalled some of those experiences Dede shared with her and Mike. "Dede used to take Mike and me to the movies downtown in DC. We would go to RKO Keith's and Lowes Palace theaters. Black people could sit at the counter at the People's Drug Store in DC, so we would go to the soda fountain downtown, order an ice cream soda, a hot dog, and French fries. That was a big deal for us."

Growing up in Arlington, white people tried to make us feel like the other. Like something was wrong with us. As if we weren't good enough to go to the Glebe Theater or sit at the counter to eat in People's Drug Store in Arlington. When we were young, we tried not to absorb the ugliness of all the actions meant to make us feel subordinate, but it made us angry as we became older. We knew we were no different; we were just people with darker skin. We were not unworthy, and we desired the same access as Arlington's white residents. Hopefully, one day that would change.

When we were about eight or nine years old, Uncle Dede took Lynwood, Roz, Mike, and me to the family day picnic at the Bureau of Standards. Uncle Dede worked in the upper Northwest section of Washington, DC, and the building was at Connecticut Avenue and Van Ness Street. We would catch the bus from Arlington to downtown DC and then get on another bus that took us uptown to the huge campus where he worked.

The Bureau of Standards was one of America's most sophisticated scientific laboratories in the twentieth century. The expansive complex had more than ninety buildings, sitting on seventy acres located on both sides of Van Ness Street between Connecticut Avenue and Reno Road. In the facility's numerous buildings, they executed tests for a wide range of technological advances from electrical, aeronautical, and measurements for all kinds of inventions.[24]

They held the picnic on one side of the extensive grounds surrounding the expanse of buildings. Employees brought their families for a fun day on the lawn, where all the kids enjoyed games, hot dogs, chips, candy, and all kinds of food as well as balloons and prizes. It was a carnival-type atmosphere that we looked forward to and enjoyed.

When most people left to go home is when Uncle Dede's work began. He was a janitor in a fascinating building. It was a role he took great pride in. During the years he worked at the Bureau of Standards, Dede received recognition for his high quality of work from the bureau and coworkers. Some employees left him personal notes and cards thanking him for the excellence and pride in executing his job.

We didn't know what was inside the other buildings, but Dede's building housed humongous round steel-looking vats. He took the elevators up to each level, got off, and cleaned the concrete floors until they shined. There were catwalks on the inner area where we imagined the employees climbed to access the equipment for some of the scientific work conducted there. After the festival, we waited in the building as Uncle Dede completed his work, and then we would take the bus back to Hall's Hill. Dede was generous and kind. We were his nieces and nephews, and he made us feel special by going out of his way to expose us to events like the Bureau of Standard's family picnic day.

24 John DeFerrari, "The Lost Hilltop Home of the National Bureau of Standards," Streets of Washington, July 1, 2013.

Uncle Dede was very fond of Roz. She was kind of like his godchild. During holidays, he made sure she had a chance to enjoy rare holiday displays that she fondly remembers. "Every Christmas, Dede would take me to downtown DC to see the windows at Woodward and Lothrop. They were always so beautiful." We loved having Uncle Dede at our house, and he quickly became comfortable with the chaos found in any home full of kids.

Now that Dad was working closer to home, he checked in on Grandma Jones even more frequently than before. They had been concerned about her health for some time. We hadn't gone to visit Grandma Jones every time Dad went, as we had done when Mom visited Nana, but when we did see her, we felt her love and warmth. She had a sweet, gentle spirit. She never raised her voice, and she was always very loving. In elementary school, sometimes we would drop by if we happened to be near her house on Edison Street. We just checked in to see how she was doing and to say hello.

In October of 1962, we lost our Grandma Jones after suffering a stroke. When she died, Dad brought many of her cast iron pans to our house. From then on, he used Grandma Jones' cast iron griddle to prepare our Sunday morning pancakes.

It had been a year with lots of highs and lows. It wasn't easy losing both of our grandmothers in the same year. Somehow, we thought they would be around for a very long time. We didn't even want to consider how difficult Grandma Jones' passing would have been, had Dad not found a job close to home.

When Grandma Jones died, Mike was in the eleventh grade, Roz was in her last year at Stratford, Lynwood and I were in our last year at Langston, Audrey was in the third grade, and Wilma was three years old. George Mason was away at college. For the older kids, we learned a lot about handling loss and change by how our parents had dealt with the previous two years.

Mom and Dad lost the people who meant the most to them. Losing your mother, especially when you didn't grow up with a father for most of your life, had to leave a hole in your heart. They were models of how to keep going, how to mourn in private, how to acclimate to change, and keep our family together and moving forward. It was a strength of character we would see them exhibit again and again. We came to understand what it meant when people said: "Trouble doesn't last always, and there will be joy in the morning."

CHAPTER 14

Stratford and Washington-Lee

Black students like Mike and Roz benefitted from the improved facilities, more advanced classes, and the latest textbooks. But those educational resources came at a cost. Racist attitudes that had maintained segregated schools were still present only exhibited through coded language and unwelcoming attitudes.

No amount of effort from Roz or Mike would change the mindset of white students who were intentionally and unintentionally exclusive. Their actions ostracized them, whether their peers realized it or not. After spending a few years at Stratford, Roz understood what Mike had been dealing with and adopted some of his coping strategies.

In Roz's last year of junior high school, her gym class nominated her to represent them at a regional-wide athletic day. She was thrilled, until she reported to the assistant principal's office. The assistant principal informed her it would not be a good idea for her to attend the athletic day. Even though her classmates chose her, Roz was not allowed to represent them. She was hurt and angry and vowed to turn those emotions into action by excelling academically. It was one more reason she couldn't wait to graduate and move on to Washington-Lee High school.

Mike had been at Washington-Lee for two years. Finally, he had a chance to recapture some of the excitement he missed while attending Stratford. At Washington-Lee, he played junior varsity football and baseball. Mike had been playing baseball his whole life. To play collegiate sports on his high school team made his years at Washington-Lee less alienating than what he had experienced at Stratford. Everything teenagers expect to do in high school was available to all the Black students at Washington-Lee. Mike went to the prom and attended Friday night football games. High school was more fun and offered access to activities and interests most teens look forward to in junior and senior high school.

Sports took a back seat in Mike's eleventh-grade year. He had to keep his grades up and prepare for college by attending Saturday SAT prep sessions to ensure he scored high on college entrance exams. It was almost a forgone conclusion that he would follow in George Mason's footsteps. The question was, where would the next chapter of his educational story begin?

Mike was always smart. It was typical at home to find his head burrowed into a thick history book or a novel based on some historical event. He had started reading even before he went to nursery school and began first grade at five years old. Mom and Dad expected high performance from him. They knew he had the innate ability to perform at a higher level, even if he didn't always do so. It was in him. He just had to follow through.

Back at Langston, Lynwood, Audrey, and I continued moving within an ecosystem that protected us and prepared us for the world outside Hall's Hill. Lynwood and I were in the sixth grade, and Audrey was a third grader at Langston. We hoped things had improved since we would soon be attending Stratford.

Once integration began, teachers at Langston continued to go beyond academics to prepare us for junior high school. They routinely encouraged us to be confident in our abilities and to not let assumptions held by white people about our intelligence become our belief. Throughout the sixth grade, our teachers reminded us we were just as smart as the white students. They also cautioned us to study hard and keep up with our schoolwork when we graduated and moved on.

As the school year came to a close, there was still one of two big elementary school outings Lynwood and I had yet to enjoy. We had already gone with the safety patrols to see the Washington Senators play baseball at RFK Stadium. This year, all the sixth graders were going on a bus trip to New York City. It was a huge deal. It would be our first time traveling beyond DC, Maryland, and Virginia.

On the four-hour bus trip to New York City, we sang songs, laughed, and talked among our friends, marveling at even the smallest things, like entering the Lincoln Tunnel. It felt a little eerie spending so much time in the darkness of a concrete tube. It was exciting at first, and then it seemed as if we would never see the sunlight again. When the mile and a half trip underground finally ended, a cacophony of sounds and a plethora of sights greeted us as we exited the tunnel.

Entering Times Square, our automatic reaction was to look up. The buildings were taller and the city denser than anything we had experienced. Washington, DC, was a small town compared to the skyscrapers and congested streets of Manhattan. Our first stop was a matinee performance at Radio City Music Hall. Neither Lynwood nor I had ever been to a performing arts venue like Radio City. There were flashing lights and sparkles all around the marquee that displayed the name of the building. If we ever went to Disneyland, we thought, it must look something like this.

Following the show at Radio City, we ate the fanciest meal we had ever had: t-bone steak and a baked potato at the then-famous Tad's Steakhouse. Up to this point, our only exposure to a city like Manhattan and performance venues like Radio City Music Hall was what we saw on *The Ed Sullivan Show.* It was a great ending to our years at Langston.

With a house full of teenagers, summers were more about listening to music and hanging out with our friends. Mike and Lynwood had outgrown the fights they used to get into when Mom and Dad left us home alone. Now, they even hung out together from time to time. Mike frequently went to the Jennie Deane playground in South Arlington because he played baseball with the White Sox, Hall's Hill baseball team.

From time to time, many teenage boys from Hall's Hill went to the Green Valley neighborhood in South Arlington to watch some teenage guys drag race. Lynwood recalls Mike taking him along. "A couple of times, Mike took me with him to South Arlington to watch the drag races. We would talk, and he would tell me about things I didn't know. Mike was so knowledgeable. And, I just listened in awe of all the things he knew." Lynwood and Mike were different, but they shared mutual respect and love for each other and their talents as brothers.

Neither Mike nor Lynwood hung out with George Mason growing up. There was such a big difference in their ages. George Mason was five years older than Mike and nine years older than Lynwood. When he came home from college for the summer, his daily life was very different from ours. He spent his days working at the country club, and then he might show up in Scott's Austen Healey with a pretty girl. George Mason would get out of the sportscar that was usually sitting smack dab in the front yard instead of the driveway, smiling from ear to ear. "Hey, how are y'all doing? Meet so and so." George Mason always had girlfriends. He and his friend didn't hang out—they were there long enough to make an appearance, pick up something from the house, and then they were on their way.

In college, George Mason started listening to jazz and we would sometimes play his albums on the record player, but more often than not, Lynwood and I would put a forty-five on the record player and turn the music up loud enough to be heard through the screen door. We would blast music from one of the hot new Motown recording artists like Stevie Wonder, The Supremes, or Martha and the Vandellas. Stevie Wonder, better known as "Little Stevie Wonder" back then, especially captured our imagination. He was slightly older than we were, and he was a big star.

Martha and the Vandellas' "Dancing in the Street" single always got us up and dancing. It was like an anthem for the summer, and everybody knew all of these songs by heart. We felt a sense of pride for hit after hit sung by young Black singers and groups. One of the reasons, *The Ed Sullivan Show* was a favorite Sunday program in our house was because it showcased many famous Black recording artists and popular comedians of the day.

The Motown sound was taking over the airwaves. It was on Black radio, on television, and blaring from our record players. Sometimes the music would attract our neighborhood friends like Charles, who lived across the street, or MJ, who lived two doors up from us. Charles could sing, and Lynwood would soon take up playing an instrument. He and Lynwood later collaborated and joined some of the neighborhood's more musically inclined teens to perform at house parties. MJ, Lynwood, and I shared the same birthday, so it was always fun to point out some of the things we had in common, including the fact that MJ had twin sisters. Arlene and Kathleen were around Audrey's age, but having two sets of twins just houses away from each other was pretty unique.

Our very young sister, Wilma, occupied herself reading books and magazines Mom bought her and in creating an imaginary world of her own. "When I was really, really young, I had things come to me in the mail every month. Mom signed me up for a monthly book club and *Highlights* magazine. When those things were delivered, I often went to Michael—he seemed always to be home because he was in trouble for something—and Mike would help me with a word. And then, sometimes I would go to Audrey. Between the two of them helping me out, I learned to read well by the time I was four," Wilma said.

Around the same age, Wilma displayed a very vivid imagination. She was always around when Mom watched her soap operas, and we were at school. We began to notice

Wilma had imaginary playmates. She talked to and played with imaginary friends whose names seemed to mirror some of the people on the soap operas. One of the most prominent ones was Gig. She would say to us, "Watch out, you're going to step on Gig."

Wilma also made inanimate objects into playmates. "Mama had all of these perfumes on her dresser. I spent hours in front of her dresser talking to the bottles of perfume. They were families, and I would say to Mama, 'Oh you can't move the *Midnight in Paris*. He's the father. He belongs there,'" Wilma recalled. Mom encouraged Wilma's imagination, and she wouldn't let us tease her. So, we all went along and sometimes asked her how Gig or some other imaginary playmate was doing. We acted as if they were real. Then one day, as quickly as they appeared, they were gone.

We no longer spent as much time at the playground. Our interest shifted to music, fashion, socializing with friends, and as soon as we were able, most of us got jobs. Roz had been working at Miss Allen's, a tiny neighborhood business in the residential part of our neighborhood. It was at the end of a dead-end street, almost what would now be called a cul-de-sac, and only steps away from single-family homes on Columbus Street. Miss Allen's first opened in the 1900s and is said to have been the longest continuously running business on Hall's Hill.

Aesthetically, there was nothing special about Miss Allen's. But for nearly every kid on Hall's Hill, it was a jewel. The store was in a frame house that probably had some minor improvements by the time we began frequenting it, but not many. Miss Allen's was safe. Even if you were six or seven years old, you could go there on your own.

There wasn't a kid on Hall's Hill that didn't spend their pennies and nickels at the store. With a couple of soda bottles in hand, you could return them to Miss Allen's. The store would refund you a nickel from the original cost of the drink. Kids instantly spent money from the bottles they had turned in. Ten cents could go a long way. There was lots of penny candy to choose from, dill pickles from the jar, oversized penny cookies, and sodas chilled by ice-cold water in the large steel Coca-Cola branded chest.

The pay for working at the humble, small, one-room store was meager, but Roz earned a little money that she could spend any way she wanted. Like so much of our lives, Audrey and I followed in Roz's footsteps, also working at Miss Allen's Store when we got to junior high school.

That same summer, we all watched the news coverage leading up to the March on Washington. The civil rights demonstrations led by Rev. Martin Luther King, the head of the Southern Christian Leadership Conference, had received significant and ongoing coverage since the spring. The stories about what was happening in Birmingham were more than just news coverage of faraway events. Ever since George Mason began attending college in the south, we felt a personal connection to what we frequently saw unfolding on our television screen.[25]

There was a lot of discussion about the march, especially since it would only be minutes from where we lived. Thousands of people reportedly planned to attend from all over the country. Roz wanted to be there. "Mom didn't want me to go to the march," Roz said. Mom was reticent about

25 "Black History: March on Washington," History.com Editors, updated December 4, 2019.

having her fifteen-year-old daughter in a projected crowd of thousands. She had seen too many well-meaning peaceful Black protesters attacked by whites in the news coverage of demonstrations.

At some point, Roz had talked to a couple of teenagers who moved with their family to Hall's Hill from Mississippi, and their stories heightened her interest in the fight for civil rights. Lessie and Yvonne shared some of the memories that stuck with them, like signs reading, "colored seated in the rear," and "whites only." Once they moved to Northern Virginia, they didn't have to deal with blatant signs of Jim Crow. Arlington had its share of segregated policies, like not allowing us to sit at the lunch counter at People's Drug Store and prohibiting Black people from going to the movie theater just down the street from the Safeway. But we didn't have to sit in the back of the bus or enter an establishment from the back door. The county still had lots of work to do to treat all its residents equally. However, it wasn't as bad as Mississippi, Alabama, and some of the other southern states.

Our neighbor and church member, Mrs. Hamm, interceded on Roz's behalf, assuring Mom she would watch out for her, and Mom relented. A group from Hall's Hill attended the march, and Roz and Penny, our next-door neighbor and Roz's friend, went with the group. Roz was amazed by the number of people at the Washington Monument. More than 250,000 people were said to have attended.

She remembered that historic day: "We weren't up near the steps; we were near the Reflecting Pool. There were so many people and all these busses dropping them off. Everyone had signs, and I guess we were just in awe of the mass of people. I don't think we realized how historic it was at the time. But we knew it was something special."

Roz started high school in the fall, and she got a job that paid a lot more than Miss Allen's Store. Once she turned sixteen, she began working at Dannemann's, a very large fabric store in Parkington. Dannemann's was her first real job. She later worked at the 7 & 9 Shop, a popular women's clothing boutique in Parkington, and then the Hecht Company, a department store in the shopping center.

Between the money Roz made working at part-time jobs and learning how to sew in her high school Home Economics class, she could finally buy or make the latest clothes. She bought shoes—Roz loved shoes, and she could afford to have her hair professionally styled. But learning how to sew was pivotal in helping her fit in and have many of the clothes she wanted.

Roz, Audrey, and I knew just how much you could expand your wardrobe if you learned to sew well because Aunt Beanie made nearly all of her clothes. She made her curtains for her house, dresses and gowns, winter coats, slacks, blouses. Whatever you wanted, Aunt Beanie could make it. She was an excellent seamstress and even reupholstered her furniture. Aunt Beanie was always there to help Roz. She guided her and demonstrated how to execute more advanced sewing skills successfully.

When Lynwood and I began school at Stratford in the fall, our interests started to diverge. We were the only Joneses there since Roz had moved on to Washington-Lee, joining Mike in his senior year.

In third grade, the teachers decided to place Lynwood and me in different classrooms, but we still did a lot together during school. When we got to Stratford, that changed. We walked to school together, but we rarely walked home together. In the years since Mike and the other three students from Hall's Hill had integrated Stratford, some things had improved for Black students. Extracurricular activities were available for everyone to participate in. Lynwood immediately got involved, joining band and the wrestling team. The one thing I wanted to do, be a cheerleader, didn't end up working out.

But some of my closest friends from elementary school, Adele and Marguarite, did make the team. Like Lynwood, they always had to stay after school to practice. We also didn't hang out in school as much because outside of lunch, there wasn't any time to hang out with friends. Even if you had classes together—and not many of us did—we didn't have time to socialize.

Not making the cheerleading squad was a big disappointment for me. I had practiced so hard. I was in our backyard every day practicing my cartwheels, twirling over and over until I was sure I had mastered the move. I could do the spread-eagle jump and the basic cheerleading moves you had to have down. I made it to the semi-finals, but in the end, they didn't choose me. It was great to have two Black girls on the squad for the first time, but I was pretty disappointed and a little envious.

I developed a close friendship with two girls who lived up the street from Aunt Beanie, Diane, and Sue. Lynwood's involvement in music and wrestling grew. He became close friends with James, the only other Black student on the wrestling team. Lynwood wrestled in the ninety-five-pound weight class. He also began playing the saxophone.

George Mason had played the saxophone in high school. We would hear him practicing in his bedroom. He was okay, but his musical skills were nothing to write home about. Lynwood initially wanted to play an orchestra instrument, but all the Black kids chose band instruments. He decided to follow suit, and he picked the saxophone. Lynwood practiced a lot, and he became good. George Mason had lots of attributes, but it was clear that Lynwood had him beat in the musician category.

While my school relationships changed a little in seventh grade, I was very conscientious about my studies, and I got good grades. I was allowed to take World History the next year. You had to have at least a B grade-point-average to get into that class. I enjoyed learning about the history of other countries and other parts of the world. To this day, other than Spanish with Miss Baruetta, World History with Mr. Perotti was my favorite class. It's probably something I should have pursued further.

It had been a good year for all of us: Lynwood and me at Stratford; Roz at Washington-Lee; and the two youngest Joneses, Audrey and Wilma, at Langston. The most significant educational milestone for our family was Mike's acceptance to Howard University for college in the fall.

Mike's high school graduation picture from Washington-Lee

Howard was also a historically Black college, or HBCU, but it was much closer to home than Stillman. Mike didn't get a scholarship to cover tuition. Dad and Mom were able to pay Mike's tuition at Howard, and because he could commute, they didn't have to cover room and board. Mike got a summer job at the post office to earn money for his books and other school expenses.

Our family was progressing. The second Jones entered college as George Mason's graduation from Stillman became imminent. Mom and Dad's hard work was bearing fruit. Through our older brothers, we could see that it was possible to move forward even in the face of challenges. If attending college had become a reality for Mike and George Mason, we believed it would be possible for the rest of us. We didn't worry about how—we just thought it would happen for us too. Two down, five more to go.

CHAPTER 15

Coming of Age

It had been more than five years since Mike, Ronnie, Lance, and Gloria walked into the doors of Stratford, officially ending segregation in Arlington County Schools. Since that time, Martin Luther King had created a movement bringing national attention to the injustices imposed on Blacks in America. His action helped to bring about the passage of the Civil Rights Act of 1964, prohibiting discrimination based on race, color, religion, sex, or national origin.

As teenagers, our interactions with white students and teachers revealed the limits of legislation. We came to terms with the reality that laws did not automatically change hearts and minds. As we matriculated within the recently segregated school system, there were hints of acceptance. Still, for the most part, the revolution had yet to arrive.

Like most teenagers, Black kids entered a period of discovery in junior high and senior high school, figuring out where they fit in. In Washington-Lee's environment, which generally favored whites, those teen years could be even harder to handle. Sports were one area where white students seemed to feel some sense of camaraderie with their Black classmates.

At last, Washington-Lee started to feel more like Roz, and many of the Black students had imagined. With more than two thousand students enrolled at Washington-Lee, or W-L as the school was commonly referred to, and only two hundred of them Black, it was easy to get lost or disappear in the crowd. Friday night football games and dances offered a respite from the frequent feelings of being in a place you sometimes didn't feel wanted.

Several of the guys from Hall's Hill were star athletes on W-L's basketball and football teams. With every touchdown and basket, their popularity rose, and the school newspaper lauded their skills. For the chosen few, when they moved through the hallways making their way from one class to the next, their eyes didn't dart between the mass of students looking for a familiar face to smile at. They were much more likely to have white students initiating a glance or a smile in their direction. Black athletes helped the school's team be a winner. It's like they were saying, you're one of the worthy ones.

Sports gave Black students a chance to feel camaraderie with the rest of the student body. But back in the classroom, some of us felt invisible and not included once again.

That feeling was never more evident for Roz than in her Algebra III Trigonometry and Math Analysis classes. Much like Dad, Roz was great with math. In the eleventh and twelfth grade Trig and Math Analysis classes, the rest of the students were primarily male and white. She excelled in trigonometry, and her classmates took notice. The classroom atmosphere was sometimes hard to handle. Her white male classmates flaunted their privilege like a peacock in heat, regularly displaying their arrogance. There were never any direct comments made to her, but many of the privileged boys bragged vociferously about their acceptance to some of the top colleges, be it Bucknell or Virginia Military Institute, one of the top schools in the state, or wherever.

Their snide dispositions and display of privilege couldn't overshadow Roz's proficiency with the mathematical concepts they were studying. Achievements like those gave her confidence. Roz knew her work was the best demonstration of her talent. Nothing else needed to be said. Her twelfth-grade math teacher recognized her abilities and encouraged her to apply to American University for college. She had planned to major in math, and her teacher thought American would be an excellent place for her to pursue.

At Stratford, Lynwood and I were finding our way and settling into this new academic environment. For us, it wasn't merely a matter of adjusting to the structure of junior high school and changing classes. Like Mike and Roz, we looked for a way to be connected at school—you needed friends and a way to feel a sense of belonging. At Langston, we had that. Everybody knew everyone else—the teachers, the students, the cafeteria workers, and the janitors. We literally knew everyone. There was a sense of comfort in seeing others who looked like you in class or walking down the hall. What gave the white students a sense of comfort and ease made us feel isolated.

In junior high school, you were lucky to pass a Black person in the hallway. More than one thousand students attended Stratford. It was a strange feeling. Walking from class to class, you might see someone who looked like you. And it's not that you didn't see white people that you knew from class; you just didn't speak to or acknowledge them unless they had become friends with you. You didn't have white friends. We had white classmates. You learned to adjust.

Lynwood had found his place. He enjoyed competing on the wrestling team and becoming more proficient at playing the saxophone. Once Lynwood decided to continue taking band, Dad went to Foxes Music store and secured Lynwood's instrument through their rent-to-own program for beginning students. But Lynwood had to pay Dad back, so he got a paper route delivering *The Washington Post.*

Every morning at six, Lynwood was up and out on his bike for the next two years. In the winter months, it was dark and cold. *The Washington Post* dispatcher dropped his papers off at another neighborhood teenager's house named Michael, who lived at the top of Dinwiddie Street. Lynwood and Michael split up the neighborhood paper deliveries between them.

Although Lynwood typically went out to deliver the papers around six every morning, he awoke very early on one occasion and began his paper route closer to five that morning. "Even though it was much earlier than I typically left to deliver papers, I decided to get dressed and go out anyway. When Dad realized I was gone, he woke Mike and sent him out to check on me. As I was walking down Lee Highway near the fire station, I felt someone walking behind me. I'm not sure why, but even before I turned around, I knew it was Mike. The expression on his face said it all. He complained about Mom and Dad, sending him out to find me, but he stayed with me until I finished delivering the papers for my route."

That job made it possible for Lynwood to pursue his interest in music. He had wanted to take up an instrument when we were going to Langston, but Mom and Dad didn't have the money to pay for lessons. Now that he had his chance to pursue music, working the paper route to pay Dad back for buying him a saxophone was worth getting up before school. Delivering papers was the perfect job for him because it didn't interfere with after school band practice and wrestling meets.

My path forward at Stratford, outside of attending class, was less defined. After not making the cheerleading squad, I didn't get involved in much of anything. I mostly hung out with Diane and Sue. They were also friends with three other girls who lived near them on Culpepper Street. Often, we all walked home from school together.

One day as we left Stratford, Diane, Sue, and two or three of the other girls from Hall's Hill and I walked up Lee Highway towards home. Lee Highway was and continues to be one of the main thoroughfares in North Arlington. It had four lanes of traffic, two going in each direction. At three in the afternoon, when we would probably be walking home from school, there wouldn't be rush hour traffic, but cars always came up and down that street. I walked a little ahead of the group, probably because there were so many of us, so we couldn't all walk side by side.

Soon after we left the school, a couple of the girls started saying things to taunt me. While I don't remember the exact wording, it was clear they hoped to make me engage with them or respond. I felt like they wanted a confrontation. I didn't know for sure, but their words were not playful or joking. I wouldn't even turn around and look at them. I just kept walking and looking forward.

I found it was intimidating. I kept waiting for one of the girls to signal they were on my side. And maybe there was some activity going on behind me that I wasn't aware of, but I never heard anything except the taunts. It was bewildering to me. All I could think was, why are they doing this to me? But I got the message they didn't like me, and they wanted a confrontation. Eventually, they just stopped, and we continued walking home.

Not long after that, Diane and I were at church rehearsal for the Youth Chorus Choir, and I asked her why the two girls did that. She wouldn't tell me, and I never found out what motivated them. Looking back on the incident, it was the first time I felt a little left of center. I didn't feel the need to conform to fit in, and in some ways, that may have cost me relationships with neighbors and friends. It was important for me to be true to myself. That didn't mean that I looked down on anyone else; I had to be me—whatever that was.

All seven of us were different in some ways. Audrey liked being in positions of leadership. Langston gave her several opportunities to exhibit her strength. Between fifth and sixth grade, she was a patrol and president of the sixth-grade class. And if Audrey had had her way, that would have included being president of the patrols too. Her teacher thought she should give someone else a chance. Elementary school was just the beginning of Audrey exhibiting an interest in leading that would continue throughout her secondary education.

Audrey also developed strong and lasting friendships, some that began as early as elementary school. Audrey and Gail met at Mother Goose Nursery School, and she and Leslie, who lived a half a block from our house, began playing together as toddlers. Later, during junior high and high school, Willie and Nancy joined her close circle of friends, which has lasted a lifetime.

When Audrey was in the fifth and sixth grades, Wilma was also at Langston. She attended half-day kindergarten, which was not something Langston offered when the rest of us went to elementary school. While Audrey racked up leadership roles, Wilma was doing well in her schoolwork, but she had yet to learn the importance of moderating her chatter. She remembers just how much trouble that caused her. "I spent half of the first grade sitting outside the classroom. When my teacher asked another student a question, I would sometimes answer. That was the kiss of death. The teacher would send me into the hall with my book. Many times, when Mom left to go home after working in the cafeteria, I would be sitting outside the classroom reading a book. It got to the point that she would just look at me and shake her head."

Audrey and Wilma were some of the last students to attend Langston as a fully operational elementary school. Langston represented legacy for so many families on Hall's Hill. Mom and Dad had attended elementary school there. And now all seven of their children had gone to school there too. In June 1966, Langston ended its role as a neighborhood school, transitioning to an Adult Education program. With the transition came the elimination of support roles held by the cafeteria and janitorial staff. Teachers often found positions in other schools, but staff members like Mom, Eunice, and Mrs. Hazel lost their jobs.

After Langston closed, Mom started caring for the children of some families in our community. She was strict with all of us, but she was caring and loving, and that energy helped her connect with children. Many people on Hall's Hill, mostly if they went to Mount Salvation, knew Mom had a unique gift with kids. A baby crying during the Sunday morning sermon would turn heads and send a sea of frowns your way if the mother couldn't quiet the child.

When Mom was ushering, she would often approach the mother and offer to help with the child. Her gesture was one of assistance, not scolding or a demonstration of displeasure. It was Mom's way of saying, "Let me help." And she always did. The baby always quieted down. It was clear that she had some energy or innate quality that could calm almost any crying baby. When it came to handling babies and kids, Mom had the magic touch. Her service as a caretaker of neighborhood children was always in demand. She already had a house full of kids, so she was selective, and I don't think she ever watched the kids of more than two families at the same time.

Dad was still working at the Naval Propellant Plant during the day, coming home for dinner, and then going back out to clean up the bank. He did this every day when he got home from work and then on Saturdays after the bank closed at noon. Sometimes Roz, Mike, Lynwood, Audrey, and I went with Dad to help him clean up at the bank, especially on Saturday.

I don't know how much help we were, but it gave us more time to spend with Dad, and that was time we treasured. We never questioned why Dad worked so much. He had less time for himself and Mom, but his actions spoke volumes to us; if you wanted something, you had to work hard for it. The most important thing was that he was back home with us.

Even though he was now working a full-time and part-time job, Dad got promoted at the Naval Propellant Plant. He moved up from a machinist to a toolmaker. I think we smiled more than he did when we heard about his promotion. Dad worked in a factory. It wasn't the kind of job you could take your kids to, so we had to use our imaginations to envision his place of work.

Many years later, I got a job working for Lockheed Martin Aeronautics. I worked in an office, but a large part of the building was a factory where they built fighter jets. It was a massive facility, and the first time I walked through the factory, I felt like I had some understanding of where Dad worked for his entire career. We were so proud of him and excited to see his intelligence and talents acknowledged on the job. If Dad had had the opportunity to finish college, his life would have been very different. He certainly had the talent to be an engineer, but I never once heard him complain. He and Mom didn't spend time looking back. They looked forward, making the best of what they had.

The promotion and increase in pay validated Dad's acumen as highly skilled within his craft. The US Bureau of Labor Statistics explained the roles like this: "The main difference between tool and die makers and machinists is that machinists normally make a single part during the production process, while tool and die makers make many parts and assemble and adjust machines used in the production process."[26]

When Dad arrived home from cleaning the bank on Friday nights, we would often spend time as a family playing Scrabble. It didn't matter that some of us were in junior high and high school; if we were home, we looked forward to game night. Dad would stop to pick up dinner on his way home. Usually, he would buy shrimp fried rice and egg rolls from the Chinese restaurant.

26 "U.S. Bureau of Labor Statistics Description of Tool and Die," Anka Tool & Die Inc., accessed September 19, 2020.

When Dad came in with the Chinese food, you would have thought it was gold. I guess because it wasn't home-cooked food, somehow it tasted better. We inhaled the shrimp fried rice. And then the games would begin. With a house full of readers—be it books, magazines, the newspaper, and religious literature for Mom—we all had a pretty decent vocabulary. But Mom's mastery of words was the best. She was an avid player of crossword puzzles. Not a day went by when she didn't work at least one puzzle. When you played Scrabble with Mom, you had to be ready to be whipped!

Mom would play some two or three letter words no one ever heard of, and the banter would begin.

"That's not a word," Roz might say.

Mom would calmly respond. "You can challenge it or look it up. If you're wrong, you'll lose your turn."

She always had words that looked like something she made up. But we learned to challenge her at our peril. It was inevitable. She was right.

We looked forward to those game nights. We laughed a lot and enjoyed spending time with Mom and Dad, even as teenagers.

It was always great to have more time to spend with Dad, especially as we got older. It was no surprise things were changing; we were growing up. Most of those changes were good, and others required us to accept a reality we would have preferred not to have. The most significant change would be George Mason receiving orders to go to Vietnam in 1965.

Mom losing her job at Langston must have created a financial strain for our family, although we didn't know for sure. Just before she left Langston, she began working with Mr. Mervin, cleaning up an office building in the evening. She would eventually start working in the infirmary at Marymount University. There were times when Mom and Dad both worked two jobs.

We had a lot going in the school year between 1965 and 1966. Mike returned to Howard to begin his sophomore year and ended up taking the second semester off.

The decision would change the trajectory of his college education in a way we never imagined. After three semesters, Mike knew he needed to do a little soul searching about his path forward in school. He wasn't working up to his potential, and a semester off would give him time to decide what he wanted to do next. We didn't judge Mike, and Mom and Dad didn't pressure him or give Mike a hard time. They allowed him to find his way. Years later, Mike would say it was probably the best thing that happened to him.

Initially, Mike began working with Mom and Mr. Mervin, cleaning up an office building. After working with them for a short period, he went back to work at the post office in DC. He had worked there the summer before he started freshman year at Howard.

In May 1966, Mike had only been out of school a few months when he received his draft notice from the selective service. It had been less than a year after George Mason left, and now the military was drafting Mike. It just didn't seem fair. The best we could hope for was that Mike wouldn't have to go to Vietnam after completing his basic training.

When Mike left Howard, Roz was nearing the end of her senior year at W-L and in the process of deciding where she would go to college. She applied to American University, following her Math Analysis teacher's advice, but she also filled out an application for Howard. Roz received acceptance letters from both schools. Dede had saved to send Roz to college, which took a lot of pressure off Mom and Dad. It was one of many ways he contributed to our household, especially when it came to Roz. In the end, she decided to attend Howard University in the fall. Her college money could go a lot further there.

Roz's high school graduation picture
from Washington-Lee.

For Lynwood, Audrey, and me, 1965–1966 had not been a year of seminal change, but it was a year of transitions. Lynwood and I completed ninth grade at Stratford and would move on to W-L in the fall. Audrey completed sixth grade and would attend Stratford in the next school year.

And Wilma's path had broken new ground as the first Jones ever to attend an integrated elementary school. As she ended second grade at Reed, she would continue into third grade in the gifted and talented program.

That summer, everyone in our house old enough to work had some kind of job. Roz worked at the post office to earn money for college, Audrey worked at Miss Allen's, and Lynwood's summer was all about playing with local bands and cutting grass. As soon as I turned sixteen on July 28, I applied for and got a job at Dannemann's Fabrics. Simultaneously, we all waited in anticipation to hear about Mike's orders at the end of basic training.

Upon notification of his assignment, Mike reported to Monterey, California, for advanced infantry training in July 1966. He later had pleasant recollections of his time in California. "I had a great time in advanced infantry training. I took bus trips to San Francisco every weekend. I rode the trolley cars; we could stay in a hotel. I was only nineteen years old at the time. And then after that, for some reason, they asked me if I wanted to go to officer candidate school."

Mike took the requisite test for entry to officer candidate school (OCS) and was accepted. Before finishing the OCS program, he decided he didn't actually want to be an officer. The army wasted no time in giving Mike orders to go to Vietnam. That's not exactly the response he expected to hear. Mike and George Mason had two very different types of personalities. George Mason had a bit more bravado, and Mike was more studious and low-key. Dad was concerned about how being in the heat of battle would affect him. Mike had less than a year to complete his commitment as a draftee. It seemed heartless to send him to Vietnam to complete his service.

Mike during Army basic training *(left)*
Mike in his Army uniform while in Officer's Candidates School *(right).*

We tried to understand why the US was even there. At that time, significantly more young Black men who received draft notices were placed in combat troops compared to white men.

In an opinion piece published in the *New York Times* on July 18, 2017, Gerald Goodwin documents a significant imbalance within the US military during the Vietnam War: "African-Americans represented approximately 11 percent of the civilian population. Yet in 1967, they represented 16.3 percent of all draftees and 23 percent of all combat troops in Vietnam. In 1965, African-Americans accounted for nearly 25 percent of all combat deaths in Vietnam. By 1967 this percentage had dropped considerably, to 12.7, but the perception that blacks were more likely to be drafted and killed remained widespread."[27]

Mike expressed surprise and disappointment when he read his orders that listed Vietnam as his next detail. "I thought, oh man, I've got to go to Vietnam. Most people who went there went with their unit, but I was alone. When I got ready to ship out, I met this guy who was just returning. He said to me, 'Man, Vietnam is something, but I got a thousand dollars in my pocket from everything I earned over there.' When I heard that, I said, 'When is the next plane out of here?'"

Mike flew from Fort Dix, New Jersey, to a stop in Alaska and then Tokyo, Japan. From Tokyo, he went to Vietnam. He spent his first few nights in Bin Hoa and then went on to Di An, which was about twenty miles outside of Saigon. The first location turned out to be a brief stop before reaching his actual unit. "The first night I was there, I was awakened by very loud shooting. I asked one of the guys, 'Who is shooting at us?' They said, 'They're not shooting at us; we're shooting at the enemy.' From there, I moved on to the unit where I was assigned and spent the next eight months. Believe it or not, I actually had a good time. I worked in the supply office with a good group of guys, a colonel, and a couple of other guys. It was a great experience except for a few times that they shot rockets at us, and we had to jump out into the bunker in the middle of the night. They asked me if I wanted to re-enlist, and I said, 'I'm not staying here for another couple of years.'"

In typical Jones fashion, plenty was going on in our home. We kept up with the news, hoping desperately for an end to

27 Gerald Goodwin, "Black and White in Vietnam," *New York Times*, (July 18, 2017).

the Vietnam War and changes in the treatment of Blacks in America. We watched closely as a new group of young Black leaders seemed to be organizing and calling for a more radical approach to demand equality for African Americans through the Black Power Movement. That movement seemed to beckon for young Blacks like us to get on board; to join in fighting the power establishment.

CHAPTER 16

The College Years

Roz Goes to Howard University

Roz and her best friend, Sheila, began their freshman year together at Howard University in Washington, DC, in September 1966. They were less than an hour from their former high school, but they felt as if they had entered another world, and in many ways, they had. "I was so glad that I went to Howard. The first day that I walked into the Punch Out, where all the students hung out, I was like, wow! I immediately felt at home," Roz said.

In junior and senior high school only a small number of Black students attended among thousands of white students. At Howard, everywhere Roz looked, she saw many smart Black people. Students came from every part of the country and many were from the Caribbean and Africa. Howard attracted the best and brightest Black people from all over the world.

Even though Mike attended Howard in his freshman year, by the time Roz decided she wanted to go there, he was in the

Army. She knew nothing about the time he spent at Howard. Without the benefit of Mike's perspective, it was hard to know what to expect.

Howard's campus was beautifully manicured with lots of big trees and grassy areas framed by sidewalks that crisscrossed, leading to historic and newer buildings framing the main campus. Buildings were both old and new, each one named for an important figure in Black history.

Roz and Sheila commuted to school from Arlington, but they didn't feel different than any other student. They met many people and established a good circle of friends right from the start. Some were students who also commuted to school, like another girl named Sheila from DC, Debbie who was also from Arlington, and new friends who lived in the dormitory like, Beverly from St. Louis and Lennie from Detroit. Finally, she had a chance to build new relationships and friendships, meet new people, and learn about new places. They all met during freshman week and developed a bond. Roz remembers thinking, "This is what college is supposed to be like."

Roz reveled in the freedom of college. Up to this point, her choices matched Mom and Dad's expectations. When she got to Howard, that began to change, and Mom, in particular, was not cheering on her newfound freedom. Dating and her social life were where things seemed to fall apart.

Mom didn't like Roz's choice in guys. The most significant issue seemed to be the age difference. If Roz was dating a guy who was a few years older than her, Mom was not friendly or welcoming. She also wanted Roz home by one in the morning from parties or whatever social activity she might be attending. That was nearly impossible to achieve. The drive from Washington, DC, to Arlington took at least thirty to forty minutes. To meet Mom's expectations, Roz would have to leave a party a little after midnight. No college student did that. From Roz's point of view, once Mom was no longer in agreement with the things she wanted to do, she made her life very uncomfortable.

Most commonly, Mom would sing gospel songs and ignore Roz. It was the ultimate cold shoulder. It was different than just singing a spiritual. She would look off in another direction, ignore Roz and anyone else who might be passing through the room where she happened to be. Sometimes we would hear her singing and ask each other or wonder to ourselves, "Is she angry with me?" We didn't know much about the ability to feel a person's *energy* at that time, and even though she was singing spirituals, the feelings we picked up were not ones of peace or happiness. It was just the opposite. Her displeasure was palpable and unmistakable. During these times, we all stayed clear of wherever Mom was.

In our house, Roz's only place to detach herself from Mom's obvious displeasure was to retreat to the bedroom she shared with me, Audrey, and Wilma.

Sometimes, we had to endure Mom's singing of spirituals for days. She always seemed to be in the kitchen, washing dishes when she started singing or humming. In hindsight, I guess that was a good thing because it meant we didn't have to walk by her in the living room. The humming and singing might seem harmless, but it was something eerily uncomfortable during those times.

Roz felt Mom had a double standard. Although I was younger, she would let me go to college parties with Roz. This new, tension-filled relationship between Mom and Roz made college more difficult than expected. For a portion of Roz's freshman year, she stayed with Luther, an older cousin. Luther was the son of Mom's oldest sister Helen, who had died from pneumonia in the 1940s. Luther, his wife, and two young daughters lived in the Mount Pleasant neighborhood of Washington, DC, not more than fifteen minutes from Howard's campus. The arrangement gave Roz some space and a little more freedom, but it was short-lived after Mom called late one night, and Roz was out with friends. Mom made Roz move back home.

When she returned to campus the next year, Roz said the sparkle had dulled. "In my sophomore year, I became somewhat disillusioned about Howard. I even considered dropping out. Things just weren't as great as I had originally perceived them to be." She felt some of the professors seemed more interested in making her life more difficult instead of being helpful.

But it wasn't just her classes. The friendships she had made in the early days didn't seem as close. It made sense that people would develop stronger bonds with those who lived in the dorm with them, but she had not expected the degree of change she felt. Some of the glow had dissipated.

Roz and her best friend Sheila started working part-time at NASA in downtown DC in their sophomore year, which meant she had even less time for hanging out on campus, and that was just fine with her. She was making a little money and saved up to buy herself a green Volkswagen Beetle with a sunroof top.

Attending Howard also put Roz at the heart of the Black Power Movement. Howard's legacy was rich in African American history, culture, and men and women who had been at the forefront of the fight for freedom and equal rights were associated with the university. Yet, that history was not part of the university's curriculum. A group of students became very vocal about changing the curriculum to reflect the history of the Black student body. Despite their appeals, the administration took no action on student demands, so students staged a demonstration that resulted in a takeover of the administration building on March 19, 1968. The protest ended a week later. It marked the beginning of Howard being at the center of the Black consciousness movement.

Only weeks after students took over the administration building at Howard, Martin Luther King was killed on April 4, 1968.

I was working at Dannemann's that night, and I felt so alone. Dr. King died at 8:05 p.m. that day. The store closed at 9 p.m., and I would soon be leaving to go home. As the only Black person working in the store that night, I wondered what the white people were thinking, but I didn't discuss the tragedy with any of them. I just wanted to leave as soon as possible.

When I got home, we watched the television coverage, and all felt numb. Dr. King's death made us feel threatened. He was a symbol of hope for a better future. What would happen to the movement for equal rights and justice for Blacks in America?

While my family and community grieved in silence, many cities across the country exploded, including neighborhoods all over Washington, DC. Nonviolence was central to Dr. King's message and his method for effecting change. The chaos that exploded onto the streets following his death was antithetical to his life's work. Dr. King's death was a crushing blow to all Black Americans. Sadly, some people took their grief and anger out on businesses in their communities. For many, it felt as if Black America had lost all hope.

For four days, thousands of people were in the streets of DC, burning, looting, and rioting. It was a terrifying time. Lyndon Johnson sent the national guard to DC and other urban cities where rioting was taking place. Everything in DC was closed for days, so Roz didn't attend classes that week.

Once things calmed down and we went into the city, the sight of burned out buildings and businesses in Washington's Black neighborhoods was alarming. So much had been lost. It was heartbreaking in so many ways. King's assassination helped to fuel and bring attention to the Black Power Movement. In the days to come, the movement would gain prominence. Unlike the Civil Rights Movement led by Martin Luther King, the young and progressive Black Power leaders aligned themselves closer to Malcolm X's message of racial pride, autonomy, and self-determination in their quest for Black awareness.

In her sophomore year, Roz had decided to switch her major from math to education. As talented as she was with math, she found the college-level curriculum more challenging than she anticipated. When she returned to school in the fall of 1968 to begin her junior year, most of her classes were in her education major. That's when she met Connie, another student majoring in education.

As they got to know each other, Roz and Connie realized they had a lot in common. They both commuted to campus, and like Roz, Connie had grown up in a small Black community surrounded by a white neighborhood. She had attended a newly integrated school and had a similar upbringing. The parallels in their childhood and a shared interest in teaching helped to cement their friendship. Junior year, they became close friends and spent a lot of time together in the education building.

In the summer break between junior and senior year, Roz continued working at NASA. When she headed back to Howard, it was the fall of 1969 and her senior year. As Roz worked toward completing her degree, I would begin my freshman year at Howard.

Roz was determined not to let anything get in the way of graduating on time. She let nothing cloud her focus, eventually quitting her job at NASA to complete her final semester's student teaching requirement.

Early in her last year, she worked to conduct her due diligence, meeting with her advisor to review her academic requirements. If she had inadvertently skipped taking any of the courses required for graduation, there was still time to add them to her schedule. At the completion of the meeting, everything seemed to be in order, and she felt confident about the road ahead.

Despite being proactive in confirming she was on schedule to complete all of her requirements when the spring semester came around, she received disappointing news. Roz found out she was one class short of a course in her English minor. Somehow it was missed during her meeting with her advisor just months earlier. Being short of one course requirement would delay her ability to graduate in May.

It was another disappointment. But she handled this news very differently than her early years at Howard, dealing with the disillusionments of friendships, the curriculum, and the challenges of growing up. She had matured so much during her four years in college, and she took this one in stride.

Roz focused on what she had gained and the road ahead, deciding not to challenge the decision. She told Mom and Dad the news and went to the ceremony to celebrate her friends graduating.

Sitting in the audience waiting for the ceremony to begin, she read through the program. She couldn't believe it when she saw her name listed among the Department of Education graduates. Roz was giddy with excitement, but she held it in. She had no one to share the moment with then. All of her friends were sitting in their caps and gowns, and she was sitting with the general audience. The feeling was otherworldly. The accouterments of graduation didn't matter now. She had her degree. Fortunately, and unbeknownst to Roz, her advisor had approved her graduation despite missing one course from her transcript.

Roz remembers that day like it was yesterday. "As soon as the ceremony ended, I couldn't wait to get over to Burr Gymnasium to see if my degree was there." She entered the gym and showed the person working the table her school identification card. Even still, until she saw the degree for herself, she questioned whether it was real. "Do they really have my degree for me?" The woman reached into the box, retrieved Roz's degree, and handed it to her. It was the culmination of years of hard work and a lot of growing up.

In hindsight, she wished that Dad, Mom, and Dede had been there to hear her name called, but in the end, she had achieved her goal and the one they all had for her.

The Road to Howard and Virginia State

Lynwood and I were not far behind Roz, but we were still in high school when she began studying at Howard University.

At W-L, Lynwood joined the wrestling team, moving up to the 112-pound weight class. He played in the band, and for a short period of time, he and James were on the junior varsity baseball team together as well as the wrestling team. Lynwood was always thin, but by the end of high school, he was approaching six feet and significantly taller than my five foot, three inch stature.

I remained friends with Diane and Sue throughout high school, but we saw even less of each other during the school day than at Stratford. We had chosen different academic paths. Neither of them planned to go to college, so by the time we completed the tenth grade, much of our designated curriculum was different.

Now that I was working at Dannemann's after school, I had even less time for extracurricular school activities. My friendship with my neighbor and friend Gwen grew stronger throughout high school. We hung out with Marguarite, Lynwood, Jimmy, and Curtis. I later became good friends with Gwen's neighbor, Shirley. In our college years, Gwen, Shirley, and I often hung out together.

Our sophomore year at W-L was pretty uneventful except that neither Lynwood nor I performed well in algebra. If we were going to get into college, we would have to repeat the course to improve our grade. The summer after our first year of high school would be the first time we did not have the luxury of totally detaching from school. We both attended summer school, repeated algebra, and secured better than a passing grade.

Roz got a chuckle out of it, remarking, "You both have to go to summer school for algebra?" She seemed amazed that Lynwood and I had to take the class over again. With Roz's math skills, an area where Audrey also excelled, not doing well in math seemed strange. Clearly, we had not been the beneficiaries of Dad's math gene.

Once we successfully completed and improved our algebra grade, we eased into our normal summer routines, which meant working a summer job. Besides, what would be the point of not working? After a week or two of hanging around the house and doing nothing, we would be bored, regret not having something to do, and have no spending money. But Lynwood made time to earn a little money and pursue his music.

He took advantage of every opportunity to play. Lynwood wanted to learn and improve his musical skills. Jam sessions with some Hall's Hill garage bands and mentorship he received from an older neighborhood friend named Delbert, who played the saxophone, helped him improve. We all called Delbert "Peanut."

Sometimes Lynwood resorted to unconventional means to gain the benefit of Peanut's more advanced musical knowledge. "I would drop by Peanut's house to practice with him. Some of those times, he would tell me he couldn't practice because he had to cut grass. When I heard that, I would run home, get our lawnmower, and go back to Peanut's house and help him cut the grass so he had time to practice," Lynwood recalled.

Lynwood would do anything to play the saxophone with guys who could teach him more advanced skills. A group of older guys in the neighborhood regularly practiced at their home until their parents had had enough and kicked them out. It didn't stop them from playing. They would pick up their instruments and move to someone else's house and get back to playing.

Lynwood remembers running after them as they moved from one house to next. He offered to help carry their instruments. Being around them and listening to them play, Lynwood hoped to learn techniques and more advanced skills. One day, he hoped he wouldn't be lugging their music cases and instead play music with them.

Sometimes he played in a band with neighborhood guys closer to his age, like Louie, Gene, and Earl. Each year, when he went back to school, he was a better musician than when he left for summer break.

Our junior year went pretty smoothly. By now, we and all of the Black kids were accustomed to attending integrated schools. We hung out with our friends from Hall's Hill and didn't give much thought to becoming friends with the white kids.

Lynwood began qualifying for regional wrestling competitions. While his lean physique wasn't typical of a competitive wrestler, he still held his own against some of the stockier guys. I didn't attend many of the wrestling matches, but I made it to one of the regional competitions.

I watched and cheered as Lynwood and his competitor locked arms, each one trying to take the other one down. My face scrunched up when it looked like the other guy was getting the better of him. And, when he took Lynwood down on the mat, I thought, "Oh no, this doesn't look good." But, time and again, Lynwood's long arms and legs were able to maneuver out of the hold on him and come back up to a standing position.

He fought hard, placing second in the regionals that year. "I had the skills to win, but I didn't have the weight and size. Most of the guys on the wrestling team would lift weights, and I did not. If I had been bulkier, I could have won," Lynwood said.

There was a different kind of energy spreading throughout the older teens in our neighborhood in the summer of 1968. After the murder of Dr. King, support for the Black Power Movement continued to grow. The most visible display in 1968 happened during the Summer Olympics awards ceremony. Olympic athletes John Carlos and Tommie Smith raised their clenched fists as the national anthem played in a gesture widely recognized as a symbol of support for the movement.[28]

The Black Panther Party, initially organized in 1966 by Huey Newton and Bobby Seale, saw increased support of Black and urban communities across the country. Many of us felt like we should be doing something to fight for our rights. We were intrigued by the leaders of the Black Panther Party.[29]

A neighborhood friend had become pretty radical and began holding meetings on the playground to create our own branch of the Black Panther Party. Sydney, who was Mr. Mervin's son, was a year older than Lynwood and me.

Sydney had a copy of the Black Panther newspaper with him whenever he came to the playground to discuss how to organize to fight for our rights. I went to the meetings because I wanted to be a part of the change, but I wasn't sure

28 Sarah Pruitt, "How the Black Power Movement Influenced the Civil Rights Movement," History.com, February 20, 2020.

29 History.com editors, "Black Panthers," June 6, 2019.

if I would take as radical an approach as Sydney and others. Ultimately, I never did anything more than talk with the group. And we never had a Black Panther Party on Hall's Hill, although we did notice an increased police presence in our neighborhood that summer.

Lynwood and I were focused and ready to graduate when we returned to W-L in the fall of 1968. In the spring, we sat down with Mom and Dad to talk about college. Lynwood knew what his career goal was, while I had no clue. The only thing I was sure of was that I did not want to be a secretary. I felt a lot of pressure. I was determined not to be or perceived as a loser.

The decision came down to the best school for the major we were interested in pursuing. Lynwood had chosen to study music and wanted to attend Virginia State College in Petersburg, Virginia. I wanted to go to school in New York at Long Island University. I have no idea why, except that I had read about it in the library, and it was away from home. Going to school out of state would have given me a sense of independence, as Lynwood would have. But it was not meant to be. Since I had no idea what course of study I wanted to pursue in college and Lynwood did, he got to go to Virginia State, which had a good music program. I went to Howard.

Our senior year went by fast, but we closed it out with a big party at George Mason's apartment in DC. He had returned from Vietnam in May of 1967. By the time he received his honorable discharge, he had lived away from our home for almost eight years. As a twenty-five-year-old man, his plans did not include living in a house full of teenagers with no privacy.

Lynwood's graduation picture from Washington-Lee High School
Lydia's graduation picture from Washington-Lee High School

It didn't take George Mason long to land a job with the Arlington County Recreation Department and a duplex apartment in South Arlington with our cousin Jerome, Uncle Ralph's son. He later moved to an apartment in DC on Elvans Road in S.E. And, that's where we threw our big senior prom blow out.

Lynwood took Marguarite to the senior prom. I decided not to go. Throughout high school, I had attended at least two junior proms and one senior prom, maybe two. By the time I became a senior, I wasn't interested in going to another prom. I went to George Mason's to get ready for the party while everyone else enjoyed the senior prom.

All the Black kids from Washington-Lee came to the party. When each of them walked through the door of George Mason's apartment, their eyes popped when they saw the mod furnishings. He had wall-to-wall shag carpet, white leather furniture, lava lamps, and cool art on the wall. It was like something out of a movie. We all had the best time, and it was a great way to end high school and experience some of the things we would aspire to have as we began our move toward adulthood.

Lynwood and I worked to make as much money as possible for college. I decided to leave Dannemann's, applying for a summer job with the federal government.

I was pretty nervous when I went to the interview, having never applied for anything more than a retail position. I went to an office building in Rosslyn, Virginia—an Arlington business district—for my interview.

The entire process was pretty rote. The hiring managers knew we didn't have any experience; it was a chance for minority students to make a little money over the summer. One of the questions asked was how much money my father made. I knew they needed this information, but I guess it never occurred to me that it was a make-or-break question.

When I told the interviewer my dad made $10,000 a year, he indicated that might be an issue. I was pretty shocked that my dad's salary was too high for me to qualify for the program. It was pretty clear that the man interviewing me wanted to help when he asked, "How many children are in your family?"

I told him, "Well, there are seven of us, and six of us live at home." His face changed, looking a bit quizzical. I went on to tell him, "With my brother and me starting college this year, there will be three of us attending college at the same time."

After he heard that, he said, "Anybody who has three kids in college at the same time needs help, no matter how much money they make."

I thought to myself, $10,000 is not a lot of money, even if you have less than seven kids! I couldn't imagine how Dad did all he did with the money he made, and I was even more surprised to find out that it was considered a good salary. The United States Census indicates that the median income for families in 1969 was $9,400. Between Dad's job at the Naval Propellant Plant and working part-time, Dad made more than the median income. It was a teaching moment for me.[30]

I got the job. I worked for the summer in a high-rise building in Rosslyn for GSA, the General Services Administration, in the Building Manager's Office. It was a great first job as a high school graduate. It was a small office with only about three people working there. I filed papers, typed, and answered the phones.

Lynwood worked at the Drug Fair on Lee Highway. He kept the shelves stocked and operated the cash register. It was a way to earn a little money to offset the cost of clothes, supplies, and college spending. Besides, Lynwood wanted to continue devoting as much time as possible to playing with bands at parties and events throughout the summer. He could make a little change while doing that too.

The most important thing for both of us was the excitement about going to college. We wanted to be like George Mason and Roz and Mike. We wanted a college education that would help make our way in the world a little bit easier. And we wanted to make our parents proud.

Lynwood prepared to go off to Virginia State with Curtis, and I prepared for Howard. Audrey entered her first year of

30 U.S. Bureau of the Census, "Income in 1969 of Families and Persons in the United States,"
Current Population Reports Series P-60, No. 75.

high school, and while she wasn't yet ready for college, she was excited about the next three years ahead of her. Wilma headed back to elementary school, starting the fifth grade.

Somehow, Mom and Dad kept everything together. They never seemed to be phased. Some kids' parents considered them adults and expected them to move out and take care of themselves once they graduated from high school. Mom and Dad expected us to contribute to our education, but they would pay for us to go to college.

Dad especially didn't want us to be saddled with a lot of debt once we completed our degree. The schools we chose had to have an affordable tuition rate.

Neither Mom nor Dad had much time to themselves. Dad continued working the same two jobs, while Mom remained at Marymount College infirmary.

I think Dad convinced Mom to go away on a short weekend trip with him once that I can remember, but she was a homebody, and she was okay with that. She would tell Dad, "George, go on and go fishing." And that's just what he did. Dad started going on a few trips every year with his friends.

He would go on a deep-sea fishing trip with some of the men he worked with at the Navy Propellant Plant. And closer to September, Dad and three friends would drive up to New York, get a hotel, and stay a few days while they went to the racetrack in Saratoga, New York.

We all loved that Dad was finally getting to enjoy himself. Everything he and Mom did was for us. They were strict, and none of us particularly cared for that, but as we got older, we began to realize we had something special. We didn't know any other parents who worked as hard to give their children everything they could afford and more.

As Lynwood and I prepared to enter college, our family began to stand out for more than the number of children. Dad was so proud to tell his friends about all of the children he had in college.

Soon, George and Idabel would have sent five kids to college. And Dad let it be known, in a very humble way, that he hoped all seven of his kids would attend and graduate from a university.

Lynwood was only the second Jones to attend a college located more than thirty minutes away from home. It reminded him of the decision to place us in different classes in the third grade. "I was out on my own, and it forced me to develop and helped to reveal my character. I think I benefited from being in Petersburg. It was kind of like going back into the past. It was a lot slower paced than attending Howard or another school in a city," Lynwood reflected.

Lynwood and Curtis rode the Trailways bus to college together. After arriving at the bus station in Petersburg, they got off with their bags and made their way to a city bus to get them over to the Virginia State campus.

When they got on the bus and prepared to put their money in, they found it odd that people simply dropped their money on the dashboard of the bus. It was wide open, and anyone could have picked money up from there. Lynwood remembers thinking, "I'm in a different kind of place than where I just came from."

The first semester I was at Howard, I occasionally rode to school with Roz since she had a car, and we were both going to the same place. But my first week on campus, which was freshman week, Roz was a campus pal and had to arrive on campus early. Roz wasn't my campus pal, and I don't recall seeing her much that week at all.

I had visited Howard with Roz, and I felt like I knew a little about the university. It was pretty exciting to be at Howard as a student. Attending an all-Black school, making new friends, and enjoying college life gave me a lot to look forward to. When I arrived on campus freshman week, I saw many students gathering in front of Ira Aldridge Theater. I excitedly walked over to a few people and introduced myself. Students were generally friendly and open. But I hadn't met too many people before I had an encounter that shaped much of my early experience at Howard.

I walked over to one of the freshman girls who seemed very friendly. I held out my hand, introduced myself, and she did the same. She then asked me the name of the dorm where I stayed. When I told her I didn't live on campus, she turned and walked away. My heart dropped. I felt embarrassed and alone. I don't even recall what I did next. I didn't want anyone else to do the same thing to me. I think I continued talking to people, but I instantly became much more reticent about sharing too much about myself.

It was a pretty awful start. I had to find a way to make the situation work. Initially, I thought I could hang around with Roz sometimes, and occasionally, I might catch a bite with her in the Punch-Out. However, I could tell she didn't want me hanging around. She was a senior, and she had had a lifetime of her little sister tagging along with her. It was time for me to stand on my own.

I met a couple of girls who lived in the city, and we had quite a few classes together freshman year. Annetta and Lucretia became pretty good friends of mine that year. We didn't hang out off-campus, but my friendship with them made that first year a lot easier.

Lynwood concentrated totally on his schoolwork the first and second years of college, but I got a job working for the Office of Student Life in the game room in the second semester. It was a pretty easy job. I only worked a couple of hours a day, and I could even study on the job.

I enjoyed social life a little too much during my first semester at Howard. After seeing my grades, I began studying more and partied a little less. By the end of the second semester, my grades were better, and I took school more seriously.

During our summer break, everyone went back to work.

Lynwood worked at the Drug Fair for the summer, and of course, he sat in with a band or played with one of the neighborhood bands whenever he had the opportunity. Either I worked in retail or went back to the GSA for a summer job. Audrey was now working at Dannemann's.

Roz landed her first teaching job at Patrick Henry Elementary School in Arlington, Virginia. Even though they didn't attend her graduation, Mom and Dad must have been gratified seeing their hard work paying off. The first year Roz taught at Patrick Henry, she remained at home.

In our sophomore year, Lynwood and I were both more accustomed to college demands and continued to progress without any issues. I had decided to declare my major in sociology. When Lynwood came home for the summer, it would be the last time he returned home for the summer break. At the start of our junior year, Lynwood got a work-study job in the Black Studies department that opened the door to a unique summer opportunity.

Before I returned to Howard for my junior year, I had heard about a job at the Government Printing Office (GPO).

The schedules were perfect for students and part-time employees. You either worked two days or four days a week and received twenty-five dollars a night—they also did not deduct taxes. In 1971, that was good money for a college student. I applied for the job and started working at the GPO that summer.

Now that she had a full-time job, Roz was ready to be on her own. She asked me if I was interested in getting an apartment with her, and I jumped at the chance.

"How cool, I thought. Roz wants to get an apartment with me."

Roz would pay the utilities and buy the food if I split the rent with her. We found an apartment in the Mount Pleasant area of DC and moved in before school started. Roz went to work in Arlington every day, and I caught the bus to my classes at Howard.

I enjoyed the freedom of being on my own, not having to ask if I could go someplace or having to get back home at a specific time. Our apartment was small but cute. You had to have a key to get into the building's front, which helped us feel a bit more comfortable. The area could be a little questionable late at night. But it's what we could afford, and lots of students lived in the same vicinity. Mount Pleasant was eclectic, to say the least. It had a large immigrant community of mostly renters and single-family homeowners who were liberal white people and young Black professionals.

One of the things Roz and I did together was to go swimming at Howard's pool on Tuesday nights. With my student ID, I was allowed to bring a guest to join me for a swim. While there, she met a student named Michael. They started dating and went out a lot. Michael would come over, and they would go to dinner at El Caribe, a well-loved Spanish restaurant. Roz talked about the paella and the sangria, and she learned how to make the drink.

I was living vicariously through their dates. By the end of the school year, Michael asked Roz to marry him. That ended my days living away from home. After their engagement announcement, I moved back with Mom and Dad and continued going to Howard. Michael and Roz got married in the fall.

In 1971, Mike was attending college in New York City. He had returned from Vietnam in 1968 and attended Northern Virginia Community College in 1969 and 1970. A friend of a classmate recommended that Mike should apply to Fordham even though Temple already accepted him. After applying and being accepted, he decided to attend Fordham. The GI Bill benefits paid for his tuition, so he didn't need Dad's help any longer.

Even though there were bumps in the road, we continued to move forward to pursue our education. I began questioning my own decisions about pursuing a sociology degree at Howard. I still had no idea what a career in sociology would look like. I found the sociology courses interesting, but I had no specific affinity for it as a career. Until I took statistics in my junior year, it seemed like it would be a good fit. Ugh. Math.

To make matters worse, a girl I worked with at the Government Printing Office had an undergraduate degree in sociology, and she had not been able to find a job. That worried me, and I started to consider other majors. I had no plans to attend graduate school.

I heard that Howard had established a School of Communications. It sounded interesting, and I thought I should see if it would be of more interest. In the second semester of my junior year, I took one course in the School of Communications. Immediately, I knew I had finally found something I was excited about. I decided to change my major. Had I decided to continue with my sociology degree, I was on track to graduate the next year. Once I changed my major to communications, it added another two years to my studies. It was not an easy decision to delay graduation, but I decided it was worth it. What good would a degree be if it wasn't the best career for me and, more importantly, if I couldn't find a job?

During the school year, Lynwood's work-study job responsibilities in the Black Studies department called for setting up rooms for presentations or discussions and ensuring the audio-visual equipment worked properly. In the summer, the job involved a cross country road trip and was a lot more interesting.

Traveling across the country from the Southeast to the West Coast and the Midwest in a Winnebago with his college friends and Black Studies professor was simple yet adventurous. The trip from Southern Virginia to Chicago and Northern California introduced Lynwood to parts of America he had never seen. It was all new. Growing up, we never had the chance to travel across the country. Our world didn't expand much beyond DC, Maryland, and Virginia, other than the sixth-grade class trip to New York City. Lynwood was discovering more of America than he had ever seen before.

In the cities where they planned to spend time, they documented stories from the perspective of young Black men and analyzed them against what had been reported by mainstream media. They wrote what they could about the Soledad Brothers and had a chance to see Jessie Jackson's Operation Push program for themselves.

Now that he was making a little money, Lynwood could afford to move off campus. He rented the top floor of a house in Richmond with three or four guys. It was your typical college guy pad. There was nothing fancy about it, and it was pretty bare, but they were off campus. To stretch their dollars, they applied for and received food stamps to help with expenses.

We were not at the finish line yet. Each taking our own route, Lynwood and I continued to complete the course work needed to obtain a college degree.

A Fourth Jones Goes to Howard

Audrey entered seventh grade at Stratford in 1966, as Lynwood and I began attending W-L. During the first few years of integration, all Black students from Hall's Hill attended Stratford. In later years, we went to one of two junior high schools in North Arlington based on where you lived. Nancy was the only one of Audrey's close girlfriends who attended Stratford with her. Gail and Leslie were at Swanson Junior High School. Being separated by schools didn't impact their friendship; it remained as strong as ever.

Audrey liked to participate in decision-making, and she had every intention of making that happen at Stratford. In seventh grade, she took a different route and went out for cheerleading. Unfortunately, she followed in my footsteps, failing to make the team.

She says she could never master the cartwheel, which meant cheerleading was definitely out of the question. In the years to follow, she would make up for missing her chance to contribute at junior high school that first year. Audrey was not a quitter, and she had a strong personality. Most of the time, you would not have a problem knowing where she stood on an issue.

In eighth grade, Audrey went on to pursue her interest in student government. She didn't put cheerleading on the back-burner, though. Audrey made it onto the class cheerleading squad. There was only one game to cheer for, but that didn't matter. She still got to be a cheerleader.

Audrey excelled in taking on leadership roles. In eighth grade, she also ran for student council treasurer and won. While she didn't have close white friends, her student government responsibilities gave her a unique perspective that none of the rest of us had enjoyed.

She was on the inside and involved in the decision making. Audrey didn't have any problem speaking up when she saw or heard something that wasn't quite kosher. We needed more students like her who were interested in being part of the decision-making process. Because of her, the voices and perspectives of Black students had a chance of being heard.

While Audrey didn't graduate from high school in 1969, it was still the end of a big and busy year for her, as it was for Lynwood and me. She moved on from Stratford to Washington-Lee. Audrey had been president of the ninth grade and president of the Spanish Club in that year alone. With responsibilities above and beyond her classroom work, she had little free time during the school day.

Audrey never participated in a study hall at Stratford. Not ever. Sure, she would have loved having extra time to study or do homework, but there were only so many hours during the school day. Audrey chose to trade that time for the leadership roles she assumed. Students committed to taking on leadership roles in government conducted business and made plans on behalf of the student body they represented while other students were in study hall.

After devoting so much time to student council in the eighth grade, and as class president, a class cheerleader, and president of the Spanish Club in ninth grade, Audrey still wasn't able to claim any bond or real friendships with white students at Stratford.

In some ways, Audrey did become well-known among her class. Even still, she didn't benefit in the same way the favored athletes at W-L did. It was an interesting comparison. Black athletes seemed celebrated. Black students in more academic leadership roles received none of that attention. Their contributions didn't appear to receive the same level of enthusiasm.

In large part, ten years after the Stratford Four, Black students still felt the need to stick together.

As Audrey prepared to move on to high school at W-L, she would remain true to herself; not interested in or looking for fame. In Audrey, the Black students in her class had a champion, whether they knew it or not.

Audrey started high school at W-L as Lynwood, and I began college. Upon entering W-L, Audrey ran for tenth-grade president and won. Because of school zoning guidelines, Gail had not joined them at W-L and instead attended Yorktown High School. But that didn't change their friendship. Other than football games, Audrey and her close circle of buddies, which now included a new friend named Willie, went everywhere together.

Leslie was a cheerleader. She made the junior varsity and the varsity squads, so she didn't sit with them at football games. Between Audrey's devotion to the student government and hanging with girlfriends, it looked like high school would be fun.

Audrey was the fifth Jones to attend W-L. Her first year there, W-L participated in an exchange program with several schools. She asked Mom and Dad if she could apply, and they agreed.

Having someone who wasn't family stay with us certainly wasn't a novel idea. George Mason had brought people home to stay with us throughout his time in college. This time, the difference was that Audrey didn't know the person spending a week in our home.

Audrey had no misgivings. For a week, Karen, an African American student from McKinley Technology High School in DC, lived with us and attended school with Audrey. It was the first time since George Mason had brought friends home from college that we had a visitor stay with us. Karen was very comfortable and never seemed put off by Audrey's large family. Even though Lynwood was away in college and George Mason had moved out, there were still five children, Dede, Mom, and Dad, living in our four-bedroom house.

Karen and Audrey shared a bed during her stay with us. The following week, Audrey attended McKinley Tech and stayed with Karen for a week. Audrey's visit with Karen also went well. While staying with Karen, she also met several students that week who later attended Howard while she was there. Having Karen stay with us turned out to be pretty cool. Once again, Audrey took advantage of the opportunities presented to expand her worldview.

Visitors came into our small house full of family members of all ages and sizes, and when they left, a piece of them remained with us in our memory. We believed they took a little part of the Joneses with them too. There was never a shortage of love in our home, and we not only shared our food and space, but we also opened our hearts and treated every guest like a member of the family.

In June 1972, Audrey graduated from W-L. Between the prom, graduation, and college, the road ahead looked quite exciting for her. She finished her secondary education the way she had started school—being a leader of something. In Audrey's last year, she was a senior class senator. Based on her significant involvement in student government, it appeared as if Audrey would major in political science. Many of the schools she was most interested in were also HBCUs, like Roz, Lynwood, George Mason, Mike, and I had attended.

Audrey's graduation picture from Washington-Lee High School

Audrey applied to Spelman College in Atlanta, Morgan University in Baltimore, and Adelphi University in New York. She received offers of acceptance from each school. The tuition at some of the schools became a deciding factor. "I really considered Adelphi, but they were pretty expensive: four thousand dollars a year. Howard was 250 dollars a semester. Dad told me that I could go to Adelphi if I wanted to, but he would have to borrow the tuition. I would be responsible for paying it back when I graduated," Audrey remembered.

Morgan State lost Audrey's application, and she didn't hear back from them until late. Eventually, they found it. But it was too little too late, with all the scholarship money already allocated, so she moved forward with her plans to attend Howard.

Similar to Roz and me, Audrey and I attended Howard together. It was my junior year and her freshman year. Audrey and Sheila, who was from South Arlington and the sister of a high school boyfriend of mine, were friends, and they often hung out together in college. Freshman year, Audrey commuted to school just as Roz and I had done.

Commuting to school with no car was always a trek. We took the bus from Arlington to downtown DC and transferred to a bus that would take us quite a way up Seventh Street and let us off across the street from Howard. Some of the sections we passed downtown were a little questionable. We only hoped and prayed that no seedy-looking or smelly person would sit down next to us.

Audrey majored in math the first two years at Howard, later switching to Economics after struggling through Calculus III. Audrey loved Howard, and it helped to know someone in your class. Just as Roz had Sheila at Howard with her from the start, Audrey had my high school boyfriend's sister, Sheila.

Fortunately, for me, I had saved enough money to purchase an orange Volkswagen with a sunroof. There would be no more long bus rides to school for me and going out to parties would be a whole lot easier now. Even though it had been hard moving back home after being on my own for a year, I was able to save enough money to buy a car.

In her sophomore year, Audrey would experience Howard in a way that neither Mike, Roz, nor I had the opportunity to enjoy.

Lucky Number Seven

Wilma wasn't graduating from Langston in 1966, but her move to Reed Elementary made her a little nervous. Granted, she had some issues controlling her chatter in first grade, but she was comfortable moving around in that environment. She knew the lay of the land, and Langston was almost as familiar as home.

Besides knowing some of the neighborhood kids who were also attending Reed, second grade was unknown territory for her. Would the teacher like her? She had never had a white teacher and had very few interactions with white people. We each had a similar feeling when we entered Arlington's integrated school system, but we were teenagers. Wilma was only seven.

There was a lot she didn't know about Reed school. But her first year there couldn't have gone better. Her second-grade teacher, Mrs. Harmony, was kind and inviting. She saw how bright Wilma was, and she made her feel included.

Wilma remembers second grade as her best year there. Outside of school, she joined a Brownie troop run by Mrs. Hamm. She was so proud of being a Brownie that she wore her uniform for her second-grade school picture.

Wilma's second grade picture
at Reed Elementary School

In some ways, and probably not surprisingly, history was repeating itself at home. All the kids in our house except Wilma were teenagers. We were busy hanging out with friends and not around to look out for Wilma when Mom or Dad had somewhere to go. So, she found herself tagging along for whatever meeting or church service Mom attended. She remembers not minding at all. "When I was little, I went to church with Mama all the time. By the time I was old enough to read, I would take my book, and while Mama was in her meeting or service, I would read a book. I was always at church with her," Wilma said.

Wilma and Audrey shared some character traits. Neither was shy about speaking their mind, and both had strong personalities. They learned to use their personality traits to their benefit. Audrey applied hers toward leadership roles. Wilma's intelligence, combined with her strong personality, formed a winning combination and qualified her for Reed Elementary's gifted and talented program.

Almost from the start, Wilma's experience with the public education system in Arlington was different than it had been for the rest of us. She developed a friendship with Laura Miller, one of the white students in Seminar (the gifted and talented program). It was a symbol of how different things could be if integration had begun earlier.

The first time Laura invited Wilma to go home with her after school, Mom and Laura's mother discussed the visit. Mom agreed to let Wilma go. Laura's mother was taking graduate courses at Howard University and probably had a different comfort level being around Black people than the parents of most of Reed Elementary's white students. Wilma and Laura developed a genuine friendship typical of elementary school students. It was different for most of us since we never had white friends, and most of us thought it was cool. Except Mike.

By the spring of 1968, Mike was back home from Vietnam. One afternoon, he pulled into the driveway and spotted Wilma sitting on the front porch with Laura. Wilma didn't only go to Laura's house; Laura came to visit Wilma once or twice. Mike didn't have a problem with their friendship, but he didn't think Wilma should bring her to our house.

Of course, Mike treated Laura with respect, but he shared his displeasure about Wilma bringing her to our home with Mom. Mike felt like Laura being in Hall's Hill was an invasion of our neighborhood's privacy. Of course, Mike wasn't in charge of making decisions in our home, so his opinion about Laura's visit didn't go very far.

Wilma and Laura's relationship developed throughout Seminar. In her advanced classes, she had challenging work, and her skills continued to improve. She was already an avid reader, even at the age of nine, and she didn't shy away from expanding her knowledge.

Seminar gave her a chance to do that, to see how much she could excel, especially during the nine-week speed reading course they were required to pass. The curriculum included a lot of reading, and students needed to be able to keep up. Wilma loved the challenge of speed reading. She could follow the guided timer, and her comprehension improved week after week. By the end of fourth grade, Wilma may have been the best speed reader in her class.

Everything at Reed Elementary was not always rosy. In the fourth grade, Wilma was president of the student council, and her vice president was a white student. He and Wilma had opposing political viewpoints. In addition to their differing political leanings, he wasn't happy about a Black girl being president of the Student Council Association (SCA).

On the day of the 1968 presidential election between Democratic candidate Hubert Humphrey, and Republican candidate Richard Nixon, the SCA held a mock election and Hubert Humphrey won. The next day the reality of how America voted was in full view. Nixon had won the election. Wilma was disappointed with the outcome, but the SCA's vice president teased Wilma about the democratic candidate's loss. Unfortunately, Wilma couldn't restrain herself, and before she knew it, she hit him, and a fight ensued.

The teachers came out and broke up the fight and asked about the impetus for the altercation. When they told the teachers that they were fighting because Nixon beat Humphrey in the election, the teachers were shocked. Wilma says the parents were not contacted. Mom and Dad never knew about the fight. Wilma and the other student had to go inside the school and talk about what happened. Neither of them got in trouble. Fourth grade had some very memorable moments—both high and low.

By the time Wilma entered fifth grade, she had a close group of friends. Most of them also attended Mount Salvation. Her closest friends were Cheryl, Carmela, and Diedre, but she also hung out with Yolanda, Donna, and Venetia, mostly at church.

Throughout the fifth grade, Wilma continued to grow like a weed. She was only eleven and already taller than me and nearly as tall as Audrey and Roz. I was only five feet, three inches, and both Audrey and Roz were between five feet, five inches or five feet, six inches tall.

As the slim, chatty, and curious youngest sister, Wilma defined herself for herself. There was no guarantee Wilma would feel free to be true to herself, with three older sisters ahead of her. But Mom and Dad didn't compare us or attempt to sway us to be like each other. They never said, "Be yourself." They just let us express our personalities, quirks, and interests.

With Mike back home and summer break beginning, our house started to fill up again. But the busyness of people moving in all directions quieted down as quickly as it began. As the summer of 1971 came to an end, Mike left for New York City to complete the educational journey he started at Howard in 1964. I was impressed that Mike chose to attend Fordham University in Manhattan. I never imagined him as a New York City kind of guy.

Lynwood and I returned to college in the fall, and Audrey started her senior year at W-L. Wilma went back to Reed for sixth grade, anxious to finish out the year. Finally, Wilma thought, "I'll soon be going to Stratford."

Wilma's seventh-grade year at Stratford brought a part of our family's legacy full circle. A month before Wilma was born, Mike had helped to make history in that very building. It was the first school in the state of Virginia to move toward equality. Wilma would close the circle between Mike being one of the students to open the door to better educational resources and her being the last of the Jones children to walk those halls. In hindsight, we all knew it was a significant milestone for our family.

Wilma took advantage of every opportunity she could during her time at Stratford. She looked for ways to apply her talents academically and athletically.

She was now nearly six feet tall and still slim. She had the perfect physique for a competitive swimmer—long arms, long legs, slender body. She was already a good swimmer, but she didn't want to limit herself. So, she went for it all. She tried out for and competed in track and field. Long jump and high jump seemed natural for her. She also competed in vaulting on the gymnastics team.

Wilma worked diligently to make seventh through ninth grade at Stratford count. She was never uncertain about the road ahead. She had six brothers and sisters who had chosen to pursue a college education. No one doubted she would do the same one day.

CHAPTER 17

Bringing Up the Rear

Lynwood, Audrey, and I continued to push forward to complete college. Mike, now a New Yorker, had decided to complete his degree at Fordham University. I was fascinated by his decision to choose a college in Manhattan and decided to take a weekend trip up to visit him.

In the fall of 1972, the now-defunct Eastern Airlines Shuttle offered a flight from Washington, DC, to New York City's La Guardia Airport for twenty-five dollars one way. I flew to New York City and caught a taxi into Manhattan to Mike's apartment in the East Village. I don't think I had been to that part of New York before, and I found it very eclectic, to describe it kindly. I just couldn't envision Mike living there, but there he was.

When I entered Mike's building, I walked up the stairs to his apartment. He opened the door to reveal one large space. There was a claw foot bathtub sitting in the open room with a piece of wood covering the tub, which doubled as a table. His bed was at the opposite end of the room. I had only visited one other person's home in New York at the time, and that was Gwen's mother. Her apartment was wonderfully decorated and had two bedrooms and beautiful furnishings. While I didn't expect Mike's apartment to be as put together, I also didn't expect to see a bathtub in the open room.

But it didn't faze Mike at all. He seemed to enjoy the barebones chicness of his new abode. One of the things that endeared him to New York City was its residents. He remembered meeting so many welcoming and helpful people throughout his two-year stay there. "Time and time again while living in New York, there were so many people who were kind and helpful to me. I didn't know many of them, but they obviously saw that I could use some advice, and they were kind enough to offer it. I loved that about New York. It was surprising and a blessing," Mike said.

From the moment Mike arrived in New York, it seemed like he had angels watching over him. When he started classes at Fordham, he hadn't yet found an apartment. He slept in his car or secured a cheap hotel room in town. To get an idea of where he might find a reasonably priced apartment, Mike asked for recommendations from some of the people he met in the hotels where he was staying. His early and unsuccessful searches sent him to the Bronx and Harlem.

Finally, someone recommended Alphabet City in the East Village. While searching for apartments there, he met a nice Latin woman, just a little older than him, who told him about an inexpensive place he should apply for at 537 E. 13th Street. He ended up renting that apartment in the East Village for ninety-five dollars a month. He moved in and immediately went out to purchase a bed. Mike figured it was just him, and a small bed would do.

As Mike walked through the store, he found a single bed he thought would be adequate—best of all, it was at a reasonable price. As he prepared to purchase the bed, he received an unsolicited recommendation from a sales associate in the store. "Man, don't buy that bed. You'll have trouble sleeping. Spend a little more money and get a full-sized bed," the man said to him. Mike was a bit surprised, but he could tell from the man's demeanor and look on his face that he was genuinely trying to help. So, he heeded the kind warning and bought a bigger bed.

One of Mike's friends from school, named Arthur, helped him get his first job in New York. Mike started working at one of the many newsstands found all over Manhattan. He sold newspapers and magazines to the pedestrians walking to and from their places of work or wherever they might be going. Working at the newsstand was temporary and gave him a little income until he found a better job working at UPS. Monday through Friday, from five-thirty in the evening to ten-thirty at night, Mike worked at UPS and went to school full-time during the day. In 1973, he graduated from Fordham with a degree in history.

While Mike worked on completing his college education, Lynwood enjoyed attending Virginia State and living off campus. It helped him recognize the real-world responsibilities of adulthood. He felt lucky to navigate the challenges of growing up while living in Petersburg's small-town environment.

Lynwood learned to balance the demands of college, along with paying bills and sharing the responsibilities of managing a household with several guys from school. The slower pace and lower cost of living in Petersburg made it easier to adjust to his new obligations.

He was now earning enough money to live on his own, and Dad only had to pay his tuition. When he returned from traveling with the Black Studies department over the summer, Lynwood completed his studies and graduated from Virginia State with a degree in May 1974.

For eleven years, from junior high to college graduation, Lynwood had dedicated his life to studying music. He had done his best to improve and advance his musical acumen. He was eager to apply all of that education and experience and begin making his way in the world as a self-sufficient young man. Instead of heading back home, he decided to start his professional life in Petersburg. He searched for a teaching position there and in neighboring school systems. Like most college students, Lynwood didn't expect finding a job to be as difficult as it turned out to be.

He searched and applied for jobs for weeks. Doubts began to set in, but he refused to second-guess himself. Even though Lynwood had been away from home, his belief and trust in God remained an important aspect of his life. His faith gave him the resolve to know that ultimately everything would work out. It wasn't as if he didn't have options; he could always go home. But it wasn't his first choice.

Just when it looked like the Petersburg job market would not be fruitful, his employment prospects seemed to improve. Lynwood received an inquiry from a local band named The Snackshop Band about replacing their saxophone player. He was very familiar with the group since they often played at events in and around Virginia State's campus. He expressed interest in the position. Unfortunately, it wouldn't provide a salary or a dependable source of income.

As his money and options continued to dwindle, another job opportunity presented itself. A former Virginia State

College music major classmate was the band director at a nearby Charles City, Virginia high school. He wanted to leave his job because he had received an offer for a position with the Virginia Education Department in Richmond, which he was eager to accept. Before leaving his position as the band director, the school wanted him to find his replacement. Since teachers often sign contracts, it seems that his contract might not have been up. After asking around on campus, someone recommended that he contact Lynwood.

When he went in to interview for the position, Lynwood wanted to make a good impression. Of course, he wore a suit and a tie to make sure he looked professional. He probably thought about how Dad would prepare for a moment like this. Shoes shined. Haircut. A crisp white shirt and a pressed suit. He wanted to impress. After the initial introduction, he needed to prove he was the right person for the job. He must have made a good impression because he was offered the position as band director soon after his interview.

Relieved and thankful, Lynwood accepted his first teaching position as a band director in the Charles City school system. He was truly on his own now. He also took the job as a saxophone player with The Snackshop Band. Life was good, and things were looking up. Lynwood enjoyed teaching, and he had the right disposition to work with students. He cared about others and would devote the time and attention students needed to grow and excel, while also enjoying the camaraderie of playing in the high school band. Something Lynwood was all too familiar with.

Each evening after Lynwood finished teaching, he rehearsed with The Snackshop Band, which eventually changed its name to Trussel. Three or four of the band members were also teachers like Lynwood. The group opened a small record store and used the back area as a rehearsal space for the band. They practiced five nights a week from seven to eleven in the evening after they had worked a full-time job. Trussel played at HBCUs up and down the East Coast, especially in North Carolina, Virginia, and occasionally in Georgia.

The band became popular and well-known among Black college students in the Southeastern part of the country. Some band members thought the chance of becoming really big stars was within their reach. They were all talented and skilled musicians. They could write lyrics, score, compose, sing, and play music. Concert promoters also thought Trussel had promise. It wasn't long before the group was on stage as the opening act for other, more well-known up-and-coming musical groups. They even opened for the Commodores before they became a household name.

Trussel's big break came when being hired as the backup band for a singer out of Philadelphia named Evelyn Champagne King. They traveled through summer months as her back-up band, eventually getting a short-term recording contract of their own with Elektra Asylum Records. All the band members continued teaching while playing with the group. As teachers, they had summers off, and they could play on weekends during the school year.

When Trussel performed close to the DC area, we went to see them play. We were all proud of Lynwood's success as a teacher and his brush with fame as a member of Trussel. The band eventually broke up, but not before two friends introduced Lynwood to his wife-to-be, Jacqueline, during one of Trussel's gigs in Durham, North Carolina. They got married in 1981 and lived in Petersburg, Virginia, for six years before relocating to Durham.

After changing my major to communications, finally, I had found something I was passionate about. It had been a sacrifice to add two years onto my projected graduation date after transferring to the School of Communications. But I enjoyed school as I had not before. The film, advertising, and radio classes interested me in a way very few subjects had earlier. As a teenager, I had always been interested in fashion, and while it isn't directly associated with media, it was creative.

At the same time, I was working regularly, going to school, and in a steady relationship. I was excited to see Lynwood graduate. And Audrey could very well graduate before me. It was challenging, but I kept moving forward, working toward completing school. I refused to give up, although some days that seemed like the best option.

I was torn, ready to move out on my own and to start making more money. But I recognized that I needed a degree to establish a successful career. The emotional tug of war often left me feeling unsure. I was still living at home, and I received my share of bouts dealing with Mom singing spirituals and humming while washing dishes, just like Roz. I tried to minimize those interactions as much as possible.

In 1974, at a John M. Langston Citizens Association event, I met Max Robinson, the first Black anchorman at the DC CBS affiliate, WTOP-TV. Max was originally from Richmond, Virginia, and his mother had been active in the Virginia Baptist Convention. Someone who knew her indirectly through the convention asked her if she would approach Max to speak at the dinner, and he agreed. Even though I was still living on Hall's Hill, I probably would not have gone to that dinner if I had not learned that Max Robinson was speaking.

It was a rare opportunity to meet someone of his stature in person. It turned out to be a critical event in my life.

At the end of the dinner, I introduced myself to Max. I told him I was studying communications at Howard University. He asked me to send him my resume, and I did. I never heard anything from him, and I continued working toward my degree at Howard.

One year later, in July or August of 1975, I received a letter from WTOP-TV, which many referred to simply as Channel 9. I was looking forward to returning to Howard in the fall and my graduation was imminent with only fifteen credit hours needed to complete my degree. The letter informed me I had been chosen to interview for a position in a news training program. I was ecstatic. I had no idea where they got my name, but this was an opportunity I could only dream of.

I confirmed my interest and went to the interview. The station only chose six trainees for a one-year training program. Four positions went to news reporter trainees, and two positions went to assistant director trainees. Three hundred people interviewed for these six positions. Gayle King, who now anchors the CBS Morning News, was also one of the three hundred interview candidates chosen for the news reporter training program. I became one of the assistant director trainees in the year-long program. There was no guarantee of a job at the end of our training, but it gave us a chance to get real-world experience and expand our resumes.

In September 1975, I began working as an assistant director trainee at Channel 9. Many years later, I found out inadvertently from the station's programming director at the television station that he received my resume from Max Robinson. I think Max had left the station to become an anchor for ABC World News by that time, so I don't recall if I ever had a chance to thank him.

When I accepted the position, I also decided to take a year off from school while I was in training. Our schedules were somewhat erratic and typically changed every few weeks. One week you might work from five-thirty in the morning to one in the afternoon. The next week you could work from three in the afternoon to sign-off, which is when the station went off the air. My work schedule was unpredictable. There was no way for me to know from one week to the next if I would be able to attend class. The training program was a chance of a lifetime, and I decided it was worth the sacrifice. At the end of the one-year period, I was hired as a full-time assistant director.

Dad never stopped asking me when I was going to go back to school to finish my degree. After working full time at Channel 9 for several years, I began taking one class a semester in the evening until I completed my degree in 1982.

At the end of Audrey's freshman year at Howard, she knew she wanted to be more involved on campus. That would be difficult as a commuter student. Mom and Dad agreed to let Audrey live on campus in her sophomore year, although she had to take out a loan to pay her room and board, while Mom and Dad continued paying her tuition.

Audrey found many more opportunities to be involved once she moved on campus to live in Howard's Meridian Hill dormitory in her sophomore and junior years. When Audrey moved into the dorm, her friend from Hall's Hill, Nancy, transferred to Howard from Morris Brown College in Atlanta and joined her in the dorm. She and Audrey both lived in the Meridian Hill dormitory on 16th Street in Northwest

Washington. The university provided a shuttle from each of the dormitories to the main campus, so it wasn't necessary to have a car. It was a very different experience than being a commuter student.

In Audrey's junior year at Howard, she had one of the most unusual jobs of anyone of us. A friend of hers from Howard named Wanda worked at a gas station just down the street from the main campus. Another young lady who worked at the gas station was unable to continue working there. Wanda asked Audrey if she was interested in the job. She gave it a try.

Audrey and Wanda wore a mechanic's jumpsuit, and when a car drove up, they went out and pumped the gas. Having two female attendants was a big boon for the gas station. It was the preferred gas station for lots of guys. They came often, and they even tipped. Audrey says at Christmas, the customers even bought her and Wanda Christmas presents.

In her junior year, she also went with the Economics Club on a spring break trip to Atlanta, supposedly to explore the economics program at one of the HBCUs in the city. Their real intent was to be in Atlanta for spring break.

Audrey loved living on campus. She felt included and part of the whole college culture. She was at all the football games, lots of parties, on the "Yard" every Friday to watch the sororities and fraternities perform, and she hung out in the Punch-Out. Roz and I could have done all those things, and we did many, but at the end of the day, we had to go home. Audrey had a different connection to campus and college life. It was deeper and richer. She developed real relationships, not just passing acquaintances, with people she took classes with.

Once Roz and I left campus to go home, we missed out on too many spontaneous moments that were impossible to recapture. We weren't there. So, we became outsiders looking in, trying to capture the feeling that everyone else lived through, and we could only imagine.

Audrey was an avid supporter of the football team, especially after meeting her boyfriend and future husband, Hayward, who played for Howard's team. Audrey became friends with several of Hayward's football teammates. She and Hayward hung out with them and their girlfriends. They continued to stay close throughout college and into adulthood. She graduated from Howard in 1976 with a degree in economics.

As Wilma watched all of us make our way in the world, she saw that sometimes there were sharp turns, hills, and valleys along the road. She knew there was no perfect route, but she also saw what could happen if you just persevered and kept pushing forward. When it came time for Wilma to go to high school, true to form, she chose her our own course.

Wilma attended Woodlawn High School, the county's first alternative high school. She was approached by an African American high school student who was recruiting junior high students to apply to Woodlawn, and Wilma was especially intrigued by the unconventional attendance rules. "The girl recruiting students to apply to Woodlawn mentioned that she did not go to school on Fridays. When I heard that, I wanted to know more," Wilma said.

The Woodlawn approach to high school felt more like college. Students were not required to attend class and when they did attend, classes were either on Monday, Wednesday, and Friday, or Tuesday and Thursday. It was an innovative approach to high school. In classes like English, each student submitted a proposal for what they wanted to study for the quarter. The teachers reviewed the proposal, assessing whether it met the academic requirements and the students would vote on which submission they wanted to be the focus of their studies.

For the three years Wilma attended Woodlawn, she typically went to school at about ten in the morning and never had to go to school on Friday. Not only was attendance not required, but it also wasn't taken. Students approved to attend the school had to be self-motivated and accountable. The only requirement was that students complete assignments on time and maintain their grade point average. Wilma did attend the more traditional W-L for chemistry and driver's education, which Woodlawn did not offer.

When it came time to pick a college, Wilma once again chose her own route. By the time she entered college, the rest of us were either paying our way (since I was indeed bringing up the rear), and there was no competition for funds. Still, there was no flush of money, and Mom and Dad were nearing the end of their work life.

Wilma's graduation picture from Woodlawn High School

Wilma chose to attend Virginia Commonwealth University (VCU) in Richmond, Virginia. She also applied to Duke and Princeton and was accepted at both. Dad immediately told her not to even think about it! They were both great schools but way too expensive, and unless Wilma planned to leave college with a lot of debt, she had to choose a school Dad and Mom could afford. VCU was trying to attract more Black students at the time, and they offered Wilma money to attend. A couple of Wilma's friends from Hall's Hill, Cheryl and Carmela, had also decided to attend the VCU.

As the youngest of seven children, Wilma felt everyone saw her through one of the siblings. "The biggest reason I probably didn't go to Howard was that people always reverted to defining me through one of you or Mom and Dad when they didn't know who I was. They would say that's Pap Jones' daughter or Idabel's daughter, or Rosalind's sister or George Mason's sister. I was never just Wilma."

Dad, Carmela's father, and Cheryl's father caravanned down I-95 South to take Wilma, Carmela, and Cheryl to VCU. They moved them into the dormitory and prepared them for freshman year in college. By the end of the first semester, Wilma wasn't sure attending VCU had been the right decision for her. Much like George Mason when he went off to Stillman, the pace of life in Richmond was slow, and the city was racist. She applied to Howard, and she decided to leave school.

Somehow, Wilma convinced Uncle Clarence to come to Richmond to take her home. When Mom and Dad found out Wilma had left school, it did not go well. I don't know what Mom's exact response was, but she probably said, "Who does she think she is?" And then Mom and Dad proceeded to show Wilma what they thought of her decision. Mom and Dad put Wilma on the Greyhound bus and sent her back to VCU in Richmond. The second semester of her freshman year, a new roommate and a new Resident Assistant helped change Wilma's opinion about VCU. She settled in, stayed in Richmond, and by the end of the second semester, she was more comfortable being there.

To make some extra money, Wilma went looking for a job. She found an opening as a waitress at a jazz club and decided to try her hand at it. Wilma had never been a waitress, but she lied and said she was an experienced waitress. Confidence is not something Wilma ever lacked, so she figured she could bluff her way through the job. The first few days there, the head waitress could tell she had no idea what she was doing.

Not only was Wilma confident, but she also had a way of endearing herself to people. Fortunately, the cook at the club decided to help her instead of getting her fired. She convinced the head waitress to show Wilma what she needed to do to keep her job. Wilma said she gave her explicit instructions. Wilma said, "I'll never forget. She told me, take the towel and put it on your arm. Never stick your hands on the top of the plate. Hold your hand open and hold the edge of the plate. And on and on. She taught me so many things that I still remember."

Wilma loved that job, and she met many people while working there. She also had the right kind of personality for a waitress position. That helped her make lots of money from tips. When she found out Dad and Mom's washing machine had broken down, Wilma sent Dad money to buy a new washing machine. Immediately, we were all baffled. "How in the world did Wilma have enough money to send some home? What kind of job was she working?" Everyone was trying to figure out where Wilma was getting so much money from.

Dad wanted to see what was going on for himself. I drove down to Richmond with him to find out more about Wilma's job. Once Dad and I arrived at the club, we saw Wilma was actually a waitress. The jazz club was packed. It was easy to see a good waitress could do very well on tips if the club filled up like that every weekend. Wilma credits that job with highlighting her ability to influence people's decisions, which later translated into a successful career in sales. Wilma completed coursework for her business degree at Virginia Commonwealth University in August 1981 and quickly began her professional career working at First American Bank that same year. She didn't receive her official degree until the May 1982 graduation ceremony.

Mom and Dad were humble people. I never heard them pat themselves on the back or gloat. Although, I can't imagine they didn't have an occasional conversation amongst themselves about what they had accomplished. Knowing them, I doubt they would phrase it as I have. It probably went something like this: "Well, Idabel, they all finished college." "Yes, George. We trusted in God, and he brought us through."

It was no small feat. Of course, Dad was proud to tell a friend or neighbor when they asked about how his family was doing that so and so just graduated. Or Rozie is teaching now. Lynwood is this, and George Mason and Mike are that. But he never did it in a boastful way. He was sure to be smiling from ear to ear when the person responded in surprise, "George you sent all those kids to college?" He would proudly and plainly say, "Yes." It was something to be proud of.

In 1975, Mom finally stopped working and babysat for nearly all of her grandchildren who lived in the Washington, DC, area. Dad retired from the Navy Propellant Plant in 1978, but he kept his part-time job cleaning up the bank until 1991. Even then, he remained active. He signed up to volunteer for Meals on Wheels, which he continued to support into his eighties.

Helping others was something Mom and Dad were always open to doing. Even when we were young, I noticed how Mom never said no to a neighbor in need of a couple of dollars occasionally, despite having seven kids of her own. They were both giving people. They gave their time, their wisdom, and their hard-earned money.

CHAPTER 18

The Next Generation

Roz was the first of the Jones children to get married and the first to have kids. The whole family was delighted for her and Michael when she announced she was having a baby, especially the new grandparents. Roz and Michael's first baby would also be the first grandchild in the Jones family. Roz taught nearly every day until the new baby was born, only taking off the week before the birth.

Roz's water broke one week before the baby's delivery. Because she didn't go into labor until a week later, she stayed home on bedrest until April 23, 1975, when she gave birth to a baby girl named Kanika. Roz and Michael chose an African name, a name that connected their newborn daughter to our African ancestry as descendants of slaves. We embraced Black consciousness, and we wanted our children to understand their heritage too.

We were children of the 1970s Black Power Movement, which had increased our consciousness and commitment to learning about and appreciating our history. It would forever be a critical connection for many young African American parents to pass on to their children. By choosing a distinctive, beautiful, and meaningful name, we helped our children have an attachment to their ancestral origins from the day they were born.

Roz felt blessed to have a healthy baby, and for the next three months, she planned to enjoy every moment when she wouldn't have to be apart from Kanika. Soon she would return to her teaching job. She needed to know that whomever she found to care for Kanika would protect and watch over her as if she were their own. It was only natural for Roz to turn to Mom.

Kanika was now the center of attention at Mom and Dad's house and every family gathering. She was a happy kid with an infectious smile and a cheery disposition. Kanika wasn't picky about which aunt or uncle picked her up or hugged her. She hugged you back in the most special way.

Three years passed before anyone else had a child. Audrey was the next to add to our new generation on January 9, 1978, when she gave birth to a baby boy named Jahmal. When Jahmal was born, Audrey didn't miss a beat. His birth was almost as exciting for me as it was for her when she asked me to be his godmother. Of course I said yes. No way could I resist having a small role in the life of Audrey's beautiful baby boy. Jahmal had a perfectly round face and gorgeous chocolate skin, which made him even more irresistible. Much like Kanika, he had a peaceful and happy disposition. Babies like Kanika and Jahmal were hard not to love.

Before Jahmal was born, Audrey had started her career right after college working for the federal government. She worked for the Census Bureau early on and later became a director at the Energy Department.

Kanika and Jahmal spent a lot of time together because Mom took care of them both while Roz and Audrey were at work. Dad retired in 1978 around the same time Jahmal was born. Both grandchildren were fortunate to have a very close relationship with their grandmother and grandfather. The ability to develop a bond with grandparents was an advantage they did not take for granted.

Children, by nature, are curious and inclined to step outside the confines of acceptable behavior, even if it is rare. If there was ever an issue when the grandkids were at Mom's house, no one was better at helping either of them learn right from wrong. Mom was stern, but she corrected and molded their actions or inactions. Mom could balance her love with just the right amount of discipline when needed.

Kanika and Jahmal knew their Grandma loved them, but they also learned when she was not pleased. They weren't likely to try her more than once. With just one look, a ruffled forehead and raised eyebrows, Kanika and Jahmal knew what she meant without ever uttering a word. They knew that look meant business.

Jahmal didn't own the spotlight as the new baby for long. The Harrises, Roz and Michael, had another baby on the way, and Kanika couldn't wait to become a big sister.

Initially, this pregnancy was similar to when Roz was carrying Kanika, except the baby seemed bigger. At seven months pregnant, Roz found out she was having twins. Up until this point, the doctor had not ordered a sonogram. Roz was quite surprised. All she could say was, "Wow!" The rest of the family was very excited, and while Roz was happy, the thought of carrying two babies was a bit daunting. Lynwood and I had been the first twins in our immediate family.

At least, Roz had Mom to help her understand what to expect. Few people would have someone to confer with about the experience of carrying and having twins. Once Roz received the news about the twins, she stopped working for the remainder of her pregnancy. As wonderful as it was, Roz felt the stress of carrying two babies around inside of her. Everyday activities became more difficult. This pregnancy was nothing like the one with Kanika.

Having twins changed so many things. Her movements became slower and more restricted as she approached her due date. Roz was healthy and the babies were doing well, but even the most basic task like bending down became difficult. She needed help to tie her shoes. Her feet seemed to grow because they were often swollen. Eventually, she had to buy new shoes, since she couldn't get her old shoes on. Roz needed to rest, and the babies were telling her, "Slow down!"

On April 14, 1979, Adia and Akil were born. Roz delivered a girl and a boy, just as Mom had done when Lynwood and I were born. Michael and Roz chose African names for their twins.

The next generation of Joneses was well on its way, with several grandchildren added to our family. Considering that Mom and Dad had so many children, you might expect that they would have more grandkids by now, but we all took our time. It seemed we had all grasped the significance of choosing what would hopefully be a lifetime partner by emulating our parent's relationship.

We didn't want to settle for the first person with whom we imagined we were in love. If it were possible, we all desired for it to be right the first time. Would our potential partner see eye to eye on faith? What about their view on marriage as a partnership? Their opinions on raising children—would we share the same perspectives? We all wanted to follow Mom and Dad's example. We wished to have the same kind of marriage for ourselves.

Lynwood changed careers not long after he got married. He decided to become a foreign car mechanic, eventually becoming a master mechanic for Lexus automobiles. Music was never far from his consciousness and continued to be present in his life. It was highly unlikely he would completely detach from music, which he had devoted so much time to and truly loved. Occasionally, he still played gigs with members of Trussel, but many of his musical pursuits transitioned to accompanying his church's choir. Sometimes he even sat in with a few jazz groups around town. And he later played with a big band group as part of an annual Christmas concert that was regularly in-demand and sold out.

Less than a year after Lynwood and Jackie got married, Roz and Michael Harris were on their way to achieving their dream of a big family with their fourth child's birth. When the new baby arrived on February 2, 1982, they named her Rabiah. She was a round-faced, petite, sweet curly-haired baby girl. Now with four kids and busy careers, Roz and Michael decided four kids were enough.

A few months after Rabiah was born, they started to run out of space in their DC townhouse for their growing family. Roz and Michael began looking for a new house, and they expanded their search to include Arlington.

They chose a new home built in an area we had once frequently played around when we were kids. It was full of trees, especially kumquat trees, and a very shallow stream. When we were kids, it was pretty standard for turtles and frogs to make their way out of that area. We would spot them, and they might be trying their best to get across the street after a rainstorm before a passing car ran over them.

Occasionally, someone might buy one of the few empty lots that still existed in the neighborhood to build a new home. Things were beginning to change, and it would not be the last time we saw wooded areas eliminated in Hall's Hill to make way for new homes.

Arlington was a prime location as a suburb of Washington, DC. There were many government jobs, Fortune 500 company offices, and white-glove law firms. Many of the people who worked for these companies preferred to live outside of the city, and Arlington was only minutes away by car or bus. As most white neighborhoods became too expensive for many families, suddenly, Hall's Hill became more attractive for non-African Americans to live.

It was nice that at least a Black family was buying one of the two homes built there, and even better, it was Roz, Michael, and their family.

The move to Arlington when Rabiah was six months old gave Roz some breathing room. Mom and Dad's support was reminiscent of Grandma Jones and Nana's help when our parents started a family. From Roz and Michael's new house, they were literally able to see Mom's backyard. Kanika was already in the second grade, and the twins were three years old, but that didn't change the need to juggle multiple balls now that they were raising four kids.

Before Rabiah turned three, Roz and Michael moved to Atlanta, Georgia, in December 1984. It was the first of many moves as Roz's husband's career began to advance quickly. Roz continued her teaching career in every city where they moved. They went from Atlanta to Durham, Northern California to Boston, Pittsburg to Mississippi, and finally settled back in DC. Roz continued working in the classroom and worked toward earning her master's degree in education while living in Jackson, Mississippi. Once they moved back to the Washington metropolitan area, the kids were older, and they still spent time visiting with Grandma and Grandaddy.

As small kids, all five grandchildren regularly spent many hours at Mom and Dad's just as we had done at Nana's and Grandma Jones'. The grandkids shared a closeness with their grandparents that may have been unique among our generation. We all wanted Mom to take care of our kids—those of us who had kids and those who hoped to have them one day.

Occasionally when I visited Mom, parked in the driveway were Roz's car or Audrey's car or both. Just the ability to live close enough to drop by Mom and Dad's house unannounced was a treat. Energy exploded on any day when you opened their front door to find little nieces and nephews everywhere you looked. It was the same small house we had grown up in, and it was filling up with kids, if only for a moment, all over again. Somehow there was always enough room. I'd put someone on my lap and sit on the sofa. Some of the kids would sit on the rug. We would make space for everyone. There was no need for a discussion. We did what we always did. We made it work.

I can't ever remember feeling anything but happiness whenever those encounters happened. Among the creative chaos, there was lots of love, highlighted by hugs and smiles on the faces of our nieces and nephews. They were growing up too. You could tell Kanika was going to be tall and skinny.

And Jahmal was getting tall just like her. The twins were just busy and cute.

The grandkids were lucky. Mom and Dad's house was a kid-friendly abode. It wasn't like visiting grandparents who had trinkets and collectibles kids couldn't go near. There were rules, of course, but Mom and Dad's house was more relaxed and welcoming. You didn't see any hesitation in the kids' eyes or their actions. If I happened to be there when the grandkids came to visit Mom and Dad, I saw nothing but love in their eyes. Each one of them immediately giving Mom and Dad a hug and a big greeting, "Hi, Grandma and Granddaddy!" If there were going to be more grandchildren, Audrey, George Mason, Mike, Lynwood, Wilma, and I would have to pick up where Roz left off.

Before Roz and Michael Harris moved to Atlanta, Audrey had married her Howard University college sweetheart, Hayward Corley, on September 17, 1983. They didn't wait long before having another baby. On February 23, 1985, Jumaane was born. Jahmal now had a baby brother. Like Kanika, when her first sibling arrived, he was thrilled. Jahmal would frequently ask Audrey when she was going to have another baby. She, too, made sure her boys had a connection to their African heritage through their names.

George Mason, Mike, Wilma, Lynwood, and I didn't have children yet, and most of us hadn't even married. George Mason was still living a bachelor's life. He had changed careers from recreation to eventually managing a large team for a Bell Telephone Company subsidiary in DC.

He had a very close circle of friends who he partied and socialized with often. They hung out a lot at George Mason's home, which he shared with another single friend. Their house was the epitome of a bachelor pad (consistent with his apartment where we had our after-prom party). He now lived in a single-family home decorated for two professional young men, complete with a swimming pool and a big backyard for entertaining. It had leather sofas, hardwood floors, a perfect kitchen for socializing, a big-screen television in the den, and just the right amount of cool, contemporary furniture.

When George Mason wasn't at home entertaining, he might be out on the cabin cruiser that he owned with three close friends. They docked their first boat, a thirty-eight-footer in Southeast Washington. They sold that boat to purchase a fifty-foot cabin cruiser and they docked it at the Washington Marina, one of the areas frequented by DC's social set. Life was good.

The year after Jumaane was born, Lynwood and Jacqueline announced they were expecting their first child. On November 21, 1986, Lynwood and Jacqueline had a baby girl; they named her Britt'ny. They were still living in North Carolina, so Mom couldn't take care of Britt'ny, but Lynwood and Jackie visited often. Mom and Dad also drove to North Carolina to spend time with them. In fact, the first week that Britt'ny came home from the hospital, Mom was there to help Jacqueline with her newborn, just as she had done for Roz and Audrey. Mom and Dad felt as close to Britt'ny as they did to each of their grandchildren.

Children and marriage, well, they both looked a little iffy for me. But I felt fortunate Mom and Dad never pressured or even questioned me about getting married. It removed the stigma I could have easily imposed on myself. Instead, I remained focused entirely on my career. I was a bit of a workaholic. I was getting more experience and moving up. I left Channel 9 for a management position at a radio station and then went back to TV. With each move, I gained more experience and advanced my career. I was ambitious and found work energizing. Without a family of my own, my career trajectory was fulfilling and gave me a feeling of accomplishment.

When I least expected it, it appeared that my time had come. I announced to Mom and Dad that I was getting married to Reginald on May 3, 1987. We had met New Year's Eve 1985, and after dating for a year, decided to get married. Reg and I had our first child on September 10, 1988. We named our baby girl Iman, and the origin of her name, like many of her cousins', was African. Like Audrey, I looked to our family when choosing a godparent for Iman, asking George Mason if he would be Iman's godfather. He said, "I'd love to!"

When I had Iman, I wasn't sure Mom would still want to take care of kids—even if they were her grandchildren. She had worked all her life, and now at sixty-six years old, I was nervous about her willingness to watch Iman while I was at work. When Mom said yes, deep down inside, I took a deep breath. I'm not sure what I would have done if she hadn't agreed to care for Iman while Reg and I worked. Thankfully, that wasn't a problem with which I had to concern myself. For all of us, as working mothers, no one existed who could better take care of our children than Mom. We were incredibly blessed.

We had a steady stream of weddings and babies for several years shortly after I got married. Mike married Vanessa on May 7, 1988, almost one year after Reg and I got married. Mike received a double blessing on his wedding day. He now had a new wife, and he had immediately become a dad to Vanessa's daughter, Evita, who was six years old when Mike and Vanessa got married. Mike started his career in insurance after finishing college at Fordham. Within a few years, the Central Intelligence Agency recruited Mike to work in their human resources department.

Vanessa and Mike welcomed their second daughter, Elaina, on June 3, 1989. Mom watched Elaina and Iman as soon as Vanessa and I went back to work. Only nine months apart, Iman and Elaina were very close as toddlers. They played and learned together.

From time to time, Dad would take Iman and Elaina to hang out with him when he ran errands at the Safeway. Everybody knew Dad at the Safeway, and the girls both got a kick out of seeing how many people he stopped to chat with while he was there. The cashiers would see him coming.

"Hi, Mr. George!"

"Hi, Brenda! How's your day going?"

"I can't complain. I brought these two little girls with me today. They're gonna help me shop."

Dad's trips to the Safeway and the like were rarely quick. He took the time to chat for a while with everyone. It gave Mom a break, and Iman and Elaina got to have their own private time with Granddaddy.

Wilma was eight years younger than me and twelve years younger than Mike, but her wedding date wasn't very far behind mine and Mike's. Four years after my wedding and three years after Mike's, Wilma married Keith on April 20, 1991. George Mason had a full and meaningful life, deciding that marriage was not for him. All of our children were crazy about him, and as years went on, he would become another powerful male role model for his nieces and nephews, exemplifying our family's respect for individualism.

More babies were on the way within a year after Wilma got married. Both Wilma and I were pregnant at the same time. It was her first and my second. Wilma was due in July of 1992, and I was due in October of the same year. Wilma had told Dad if she had a boy, she was going to name him after Dad's father, Orze. By doing so, Wilma made sure Dad's father's name would remain a recent part of our family's history. I never heard Dad say anything about it specifically, but I'm sure it made him feel proud. Wilma's son Zane was the last grandchild to be born on December 3, 1997, but I had my last baby before that happened.

Two months after Orze was born on July 5, 1992, I gave birth to Maya on September 29. In the coming years, Orze and Maya would grow very close. When they were in elementary school, I loved that they would talk about esoteric things like going to college at the Sorbonne in Paris and other eclectic topics. I'm not sure where those ideas came from, but it was always fun to hear them talk about their future from a very young age. The names of the last three grandchildren were not traditional, nor were they of African descent. I don't think we consciously decided not to give them African names; I think we simply picked a name we liked.

Mom took care of Orze when Wilma returned to work, and she helped me out when I needed it. Many things had changed for my new family and me, making it challenging to have Mom watch Maya while Reg and I were working. We lived in DC, and my office, which had been initially in Alexandria, Virginia, had moved to DC. I had to figure out how to get Iman to our neighborhood school and picked up at the end of the school day while having someone take care of our new baby when I went back to work. As much as I wanted Mom to care for Maya, it just wasn't practical.

Finding someone other than Mom to fill that void was my only solution.

Our children grew up together. Some of us moved to other states around the country over the years. After relocating to advance our careers, for the most part, we all ended up back in either DC, Virginia, or Maryland.

Mom and Dad saw the future unfolding through their thirteen grandchildren. Dad had seen his dream of a college education for each of his children become a reality. And although he wouldn't get to see all of his grandchildren attend or graduate from college, Mom did. So far, ten grandchildren had undergraduate college degrees. We did not doubt that when the time was right, the other two would complete the college education they had begun, following in the footsteps of Mike and me. Zane, the youngest of the grandchildren, is on track to complete his undergraduate studies soon.

Mom and Dad instilled their values, morals, and the importance of higher education within each of us. We passed it on. Among the Jones kids, two of us also had pursued and received graduate degrees. So far, several of our children, Mom and Dad's grandkids, had done the same with five master's degrees received as of 2020, one PhD, and another master's degree in the process.

The children of the Jones grandchildren were already moving in the same direction. Jahmal's daughter was the first great-grandchild to enter college in September 2020. Kanika's two daughter's and her son, Rabiah's son, Evita's daughter, and Jumaane's son, ranging from two to fifteen years old, have a little way to go, but we have no doubt they will embrace Dad and Mom's *and* our thinking about the importance of a college education.

Mom and Dad passed the baton to the seven of us. They made sacrifices and raised us to be people of good character who would live by the Golden Rule: "Do unto others as you would have them do unto you." Education was of significant importance to our parents, but I believe a person's character was most important to them. Ultimately, they believed in living life with dignity, respect, authenticity, and love.[31]

George and Idabel Jones set out to give us the best life they could. It's something they were committed to from the moment they consummated their union. They were always in agreement on how to raise their children. Don't get me wrong—they had their little tit-for-tat discussions, but they never disagreed on how to raise us. I can't remember one time in my entire life ever hearing my parents argue. Never. For us, they were the example of a good marriage and great parents.

Mom and Dad in their late 80's and 90's

31 Matthew 7:12, King James Version.

We didn't have everything, and we weren't immune to the sadness and disappointment kids can sometimes feel when parents aren't able to give them some of the material things their friends receive. Learning to not let those things consume us taught us at an early age how to handle disappointment and keep going forward. We learned material things were not a substitute for real love.

As adults, with the benefit of hindsight and perspective, we recognize the value of those more difficult moments. It didn't always feel good experiencing them, but so much else about our lives was good. Mom and Dad helped us to become adults with an appreciation and aspiration to be men and women of good character. This quality sustains us and has established a model for the next generation. The fifth chapter of Romans, verses three through five, is an apt scripture that I believe sums up much about their lives, how they raised us, and how we are raising our children.

Romans 5:3-5

Not only so, but we also glory in our sufferings, because we know that suffering produces perseverance; perseverance, character; and character, hope.

And hope does not put us to shame, because God's love has been poured out into our hearts through the Holy Spirit, who has been given to us.[32]

32 Romans 5:3-5, New International Version.

ACKNOWLEDGMENTS

This book would not be possible without the help and support of my brothers and sisters, George (George Mason), Michael (Mike), Rosalind (Roz), Lynwood, Audrey, and Wilma. Every interview and discussion we shared inspired and reminded me to capture each voice and experience in our collective story—and most of all, to make them proud. Thank you for trusting me to tell our family's story.

Reginald, my understanding and supportive husband, gave me space and time to devote countless hours over the last ten months to writing, researching, and editing this book. I am forever grateful for your love and encouragement. Thank you to my daughters, Iman and Maya, for being early beta readers, offering a young adult perspective, and believing in me from the start.

Eric Koester, you and your innovative Creator Institute made it possible to take a long-held desire and translate it into a reality, and all within a year. I am forever indebted to you for sharing your gift with me.

Thank you to Brian Bries and New Degree Press for supporting the publication of my book and your enlightenment and direction in the publishing process. To the New Degree Press editing team, Jemiscoe Chambers-Black and Kendra Kadam, you were both fantastic!

Jemiscoe, you made me such a better writer, expanded my knowledge of the craft, and encouraged me to stretch, research, and learn more about the art of writing a book. Each week, I looked forward to our sessions with anticipation and angst, knowing I needed to step up my game and that you were always there to encourage me and guide me.

Kendra, thank you for all your support and compassion. Who knew the editing process would be as (maybe more) painful than the writing and creating? You kept me going, encouraged me when I wasn't sure I would see the finish line, and reminded me that my book was worth sharing with the world.

Thank you to everyone who believed in me, a first-time author, and supported me by pre-ordering my book through my Indiegogo campaign.

Josephine Alexander
Tallulah Anderson
Ingrid Antonio
Walter M. Baker
Carolyn Baker Nelson
Richard Barker
Robin Beaman
Christina Bennett
Christy Bennett
Diane Blankumsee
Deborah Branch
John M. Brown
Alan Bruner
Wanda J. Walker-Burnette
Paula Caffey
Belinda Caraballo
Angela Cauthorn
Dee Chambliss
Reginald Cole
Christina Cole
Maya Cole
Iman Cole
Ryan P. Conner
Audrey Corley
Jumaane Corley
Warren Craddock
Denni Cravins
LaNae Croxton
Taunya Curry
Janice Dade

Melissa Daley
Dedra Dawson
Rosalyn Doaks
Annette Donfor
Deborah Dudley
Lydia Eady Davis
Cynthia Featherson
Eileen Ferré
Pat Flannagan
Maurita Coley Flippin
Janine Fondon
Gloria Ford
Kimberly Lacey Foster
Joslin Gallatin
Roger Glass
Sonya Goins
Marguarite Gooden
Ava Hall
Sandy Halmon
Sabrina Hamilton
Stephanie Hamm
Daisette Harmon
Akil Harris
Rabiah Harris
Michael B. Harris
Darryl Heggans
Allison B. Herbert
Verna Holtzclaw
Cynthia Holuta
Angela Hope
Theresa Howard
Jihan Howard
Jerry Jackson
Fred Johnson
Dania Jolley
Michael Jones
Britt'ny Jones
George Jones Jr
Lynwood N. Jones
Wilma Jones
Cheryl Kannepalli
Monica Keen
John Kent
Eric Koester
Anthony Lacey
Jack Lambert
Leroy Lattimore II
Darian Lawrence
Mark Leach
Jeff Lee
Julian Lewis
Sita Lewis

Delores E. Little
Annie Lorenzana
Marsha Lyons
Rhonda Lyttle Smith
Gwen McKinsey
Doris McMillon
Vicki McPhaul
Montez Miller
Charles Montgomery
Belinda Moyer
Patricia Neverson
Derek Newton
Gail Neylan
Jessica Pantages
Sharon Pelham
Scott Perkins
Renita Price
Gary L. Price
Sylvia Reis
Nora Richardson
Jean Riggins
David Ruffner
Marshall Ruffner
Monique Sadler
Dana Schenck
Tiffany Simon
Cookie Southern
Sue Ann Staake-Wayne
Patt Stevens
Kitty Clark Stevenson
Reese Stone
Jill Strachan-Batson
Richard Stuart Perkins
Nazziwa Teddy
Kanika Thelwell
Gloria Thompson
Lillian Thompson
Marsha Tucker
Stephanie Valadez
Dr. Cherie Ward
Aja White
Deborah Williams
Tressa and Bruce Williams
Warren Williams

APPENDIX

AUTHORS NOTE

Liebertz, John. *A Guide to African American Heritage of Arlington County, Virginia.* Arlington: Arlington Department of Community Planning, Housing and Development Historic Preservation Program, 2016.

CHAPTER 1: GIVING THANKS

Rummel, Rachel. "Chitlins." Atlas Obsura: Gastro Obscura. Accessed September 19, 2020. https://www.atlasobscura.com/foods/chitlins-american-south.

CHAPTER 2: THE GREENE FAMILY

United States Legislative Information. *Race Relations in the 1930s and 1940s.* Library of Congress. Accessed October 1, 2020. https://www.loc.gov/classroom-materials/united-states-history-primary-source-timeline/great-depression-and-world-war-ii-1929-1945/race-relations-in-1930s-and-1940s/.

CHAPTER 3: THE JONESES

Jones, Wilma. My Halls Hill Family: More Than a Neighborhood. New Providence: Bowker, October 10, 2018.

CHAPTER 4: NANA'S HOUSE

D.C. Sgt. Engineer Foreman in France.

Library of Congress. *Today in History—April 8: Works Progress Administration.* Accessed October 1, 2020. https://www.loc.gov/item/today-in-history/april-08/.

Liebertz, John. *A Guide to African American Heritage of Arlington County, Virginia.* Arlington: Arlington Department of Community Planning, Housing and Development Historic Preservation Program, Second Edition 2016.

CHAPTER 6: BE FRUITFUL AND MULTIPLY

U.S. Department of Commerce, U.S. Census Bureau. *The Baby Boom Cohort in the United States: 2012 to 2060,* by Colby, Sandra L. and Jennifer M. Ortman. Washington, D.C., 2014. https://www.census.gov/prod/2014pubs/p25-1141.pdf.

Shaver, Lee. "Crossing the Divide." Arlington Magazine, October 15, 2013. https://www.arlingtonmagazine.com/crossing-the-divide/.

CHAPTER 7: LANGSTON ELEMENTARY SCHOOL

McCaffrey, Scott. "Principal of Arlington's Segregated Black High School Dies at 102." *Inside NOVA*, June 19, 2015.

CHAPTER 9: THE COUNTRY CLUB

Babin, Patricia Kuhn. Links to the Past: A Historic Resource Study of National Park Service Golf Courses in the District of Columbia. United States: National Park Service Division of Publications, 2018.

Burchard, Hank. "Hall's Hill: Blacks Hold the High Ground." *The Washington Post*, February 27, 1969.

Washington Golf and Country Club, "History." Accessed September 19, 2020. https://www.washingtongolfcc.org/History.

CHAPTER 10: BECOMING THE STRATFORD FOUR

Bestebreurtje, Lindsey. "Built by People Themselves – African American Community Development in Arlington, Virginia, From Civil War to Civil Rights." (PhD diss., George Mason University, 2017).

Jones, Wilma. *My Halls Hill Family: More Than a Neighborhood.* New Providence: Bowker. October 10, 2018.

Werner, Mary Lou. *"Arlington's School Case Heard, 30 Negroes Seek to Enter Seven White Institutions."* The Evening Star. September 2, 1958.

Werner, Mary Lou. *"Must Enroll Students in January '59: Board's Rejection of 26 Others Upheld by Bryan."* The Evening Star. September 17, 1958.

CHAPTER 12: THE FIRST JONES ATTENDS COLLEGE

NAACP Legal Defense and Educational Fund. Scholarship Recipients: Vivian Malone Jones. Accessed September 29, 2020. https://www.naacpldf.org/about-us/scholarship-recipients/vivian-malone-jones/.

Jones, Wilma. *My Halls Hill Family: More Than a Neighborhood.* New Providence: Bowker, October 10, 2018.

CHAPTER 13: LOSING THE ONES WE LOVE

DeFerrari, John. "Streets of Washington." The Lost Hilltop Home of the National Bureau of Standards, July 1, 2013. http://www.streetsofwashington.com/2013/07/the-lost-hilltop-home-of-national.html. <bibliography>

Washington Navy Yard, Human Resources Office. History of the Washington Navy Yard Civilian Workforce 1799-1962, by John G. Sharp. Washington, D.C., 2003.

CHAPTER 14: STRATFORD AND WASHINGTON-LEE

History.com Editors. *Black History: March on Washington.* Updated December 4, 2019. https://www.history.com/topics/black-history/march-on-washington.

CHAPTER 15: COMING OF AGE

Anka Tool & Die Inc., "U.S. Bureau of Labor Statistics Description of Tool and Die," accessed September 19, 2020. http://www.ankatool.com/labour.html.

CHAPTER 16: THE COLLEGE YEARS

Pruitt, Sarah. "How the Black Power Movement Influenced the Civil Rights Movement." History.com, February 20, 2020.

U.S. Bureau of the Census. *"Income in 1969 of Families and Persons in the United States."* Current Population Reports Series P-60, No. 75. https://www2.census.gov/library/publications/1970/demographics/p60-75.pdf.

CPSIA information can be obtained
at www.ICGtesting.com
Printed in the USA
BVHW080006231220
596003BV00007B/166

9 781636 766027